How To Make Millions

When Thousands Have Been Laid Off!
7 Success Profiles from Self-Made Millionaires
Featuring an Exclusive Interview with
Stedman Graham on Leadership

By: Philippe Matthews

WHY I WROTE THIS BOOK

Okay, I know what you're saying, "Another wealth-building book, right?" Wrong. This book is not about me being an expert to you. This book is about How To Make Millions When Thousands Have Been Laid Off and the seven self-made millionaires presenting their unique viewpoints and methods of wealth building.

I must have read over a thousand books, and have been inspired by several philosophies on the idea of becoming a self-made millionaire. I thought it would be best if I let the experts tell you, in their own words how they did it, and how you can too. Therefore, it is my mission with How To Make Millions When Thousands Have Been Laid Off to have your paradigms shifted and possibly your current beliefs challenged as it relates to wealth accumulation before, during and after a job or income loss.

This book is about changing your mindset as it relates to money and wealth accumulation. This book is about creating new paradigms as it relates to financial security vs. financial freedom. Bob Proctor, Les Brown, Robert G. Allen, Dr. Cuttie Bacon III, Robert Kiyosaki, Joseph Janiczek, Brian Tracy and Leadership Mentor, Stedman Graham, are all self-made millionaires and all of them have mindsets that are similar. Secondly, they've all appeared on the *Philippe Matthews Show*, and I have been interviewing most of them for the past 20 and know their integrity as it relates to making, multiplying and managing money.

They all worked smart to achieve wealth. They all add value to people's lives with their products and services. They are generous, gift-giving people and they don't buy into the belief that money and wealth are limited to only a chosen few. They do believe that a layoff is nothing more than a reason to look up at new possibilities.

As you read this book and delve into the personal profiles of these self-made millionaires, I'd like for you to identify the dominant beliefs that drove each of them to financial freedom and find out how these teachers can teach you how to become a self-made millionaire. For example, Bob Proctor will teach you how to believe in yourself and know that prosperity and wealth is your divine birthright. He will help you understand his philosophy of being born rich. In his book with the same title, Bob says,, "...*before any of us can even begin to overcome the poverty which surrounds us in our external world, we must first conquer the impoverishment that is buried deep within ourselves.*"

For more than two decades, I've had the privilege to interview a man known as Mamie Brown's Baby Boy, <u>Les Brown</u>; and with each interview it has been, "*A plumb, pleasing privilege as well as a pleasure!*" As a renowned professional speaker, author and television personality, Les Brown has risen to national prominence by delivering a high-energy message, which tells people how to shake off mediocrity and live up to their greatness. It is a message Les Brown has learned from his own life and one he is helping others apply to their lives. In this book, Les will talk about how to begin believing that wealth is possible for you because there was a time when he didn't believe it himself. He says, "Among the easiest things I've ever done was to earn a million dollars; but the most difficult thing that I've ever had to overcome was to believe that it could happen to me. That's the real challenge. The bottom line is when we start talking about wealth, there's a little known secret that most never get. You don't get in life what you want; you get out of life on what you are, and that's why we must invest in ourselves."

Robert Kiyosaki will help you understand the four mentalities of people and how they make their money. His best-selling book and audio series, <u>Rich Dad, Poor Dad</u>, will literally stop you in your tracks and challenge every single misconception you had about money and creating wealth. In his profile, you will find out why people literally numb themselves to financial gain and opportunity and why they have been so conditioned to think that life and attaining wealth is difficult. Robert will also help you learn how your formal education may have stifled you from becoming wealthy by conditioning or programming you to work for someone else for a living rather than living your life's work. Robert says, *"The main reason people struggle financially, is because they spent years in school but learned nothing about money. The result is people learn to work for money...but never learn how to have money work for them."*

If someone told you, *"You Can Have Absolute Financial Freedom."* What would you think? How would you respond to the thought of being financially free? What does that mean to you, your spouse, and your family? Well, Joseph J. Janiczek, MSFS, ChFC is President of *Janiczek & Company, LTD.*, a leading Financial Advisory Firm based in Greenwood Village, Colorado, specializes in the complex investment, income tax and estate planning needs of individuals on the path to achieving absolute financial freedom. This financial genius says that mistakes are great moments*! "The idea is to grow and to take action. However, to take action, you are going to make mistakes from time to time and you can have your greatest learning experiences by making mistakes like most of us do. If we are brought up thinking that mistakes are bad, we basically put ourselves in financial stagnation because we don't take action."*

Years ago, I purchased *The Psychology of Achievement*, by Brian Tracy, and found my life forever changed. Brian's principles about wealth, success and achievement are mind-bending and guaranteed to change your life. A preview of Brian's wisdom comes from this quote: "Success leaves tracks. If you want to be successful, find out not only what other successful people do, but find out how other successful people think." This is literally what How To Make Millions When Thousands Have Been Laid Off is all about, finding out how the rich and prosperous think and by simulating their mindset, you will be able to duplicate the process of wealth in your life as well.

I'm honored to know Dr. Cuttie Bacon III, the man who wrote the book, *How To Teach Kids to Be Millionaires*. Dr. Bacon teaches children and their parents how to be millionaires using proven methods of strategic wealth building. Dr. Bacon's financial prowess is eloquently summarized when he says, *"It's important to save one to two dollars a day for your child because one, it's a model experience. You are modeling for the child what he or she should do with money. Most parents know how to give a child a dollar or two a day, and let them spend it on useless things like candy, gum and junk. When you constantly do that for twelve years, children grow up believing that a dollar or two has little or no value and the only possible thing to do with it is to race to the drugstore and spend it."*

Author of Multiple Streams of Income, millionaire maker Robert G. Allen bounced right back with another best-seller, **Multiple Streams** of Internet Income and the *One Minute Millionaire*, which has become my Internet marketing bible. Robert's philosophy of starting a business with little or no money down will teach you how to truly be an entrepreneur. If you only use one paragraph of the principles he espouses in this book, you will be able to greatly transform your life! Until I read Robert's book and applied his principles, I floundered helplessly trying to make money with my dotcom. However, it was the interview that I am sharing with you in this book that helped change my view on self-made millionaires. Robert said: *"The source of all wealth is God. God knows where the gold is. You can't create wealth by yourself without having tapped into the source that knows what stocks are going up tomorrow, which pieces of real estate are going to be more valuable, which businesses have the best chance of success — you need to be tapped in. The way I do that is tithing..."* That statement, and the rest of his interview, had a profound affect on me, as it will you. Read Robert Allen's profile and see for yourself why they call him the Millionaire Master.

Finally, the exclusive feature interview with Stedman Graham. Before you can create wealth, you must have leadership skills and who better to teach us the importance of leadership than the man who personifies the very essence of leadership. After interviewing Stedman Graham, the author of three bestselling books, *You Can Make It Happen*, *Teens Can Make It Happen* and *Build Your Own Life Brand*, I quickly discovered that he is a master of strategic planning and leadership. In the special chapter dedicated to him, he will show you the process of reinventing yourself to be a leader; so you can be prepared for success and wealth when it happens. Stedman emphasized, *"Cultivating leadership qualities is really an investment in self. It's about leading, managing and controlling yourself in such a way that other people see your example and aspire to where you're going."* Stedman will show you that it's not about selling a product or service; it's about becoming the product or service.

The individuals profiled in this book literally changed my life and I'm certain they will do the same for you. Don't focus on one; absorb the teachings and philosophy of all of the profiles in How To Make Millions When Thousands Have Been Laid Off. I am truly fortunate to have interviewed some of the greatest minds in the world and since been labeled, the "*Oprah of Internet*" by Mark Victor Hansen. Nevertheless, I'm even more fortunate to be in a position to offer you these interviews that will forever change your financial life.

Enjoy!

Proceeds from the sale of this book go to the HOW Movement.
(*www.howmovement.org*)

TABLE OF CONTENTS

FOREWORD

The Reverend Doctor Johnnie Colemon

Pay NO attention to the puny headlines of the day. Focus ALL your attention on your Eternal Strengths and Divine Purpose.

The reason you are reading this book is because you are exceptional. You have decided not to be part of the crowd that is driven by the hysteria of the moment. Of course, there are layoffs and downsizing of certain man-made enterprises. That is a result of their consciousness, their state of mind, their inner and outer awareness. Because they believe there are "difficult times" ahead for their businesses, they plan for scarcity. The laws of the universe are just and fair, and reward them with the scarcity that they had planned to experience.

But, as I tell my congregation, and am now telling you: YOU ARE DIFFERENT. You know that if one door is closing, it is because another one is opening. You know that it is the Divine Will that you and every individual on the face of this earth should live a healthy, happy, and prosperous life. You know that there is a dream in your heart, which will bless the world. Just think of it, you may have a dream, a deep God-given desire to operate a business. This business, when fully developed, will provide high quality products and services. This business will pay fair wages and bonuses. Your associates will have good housing, send their children to good schools, and become leaders in their churches and communities. All people affected by your business will enjoy happy, healthy, prosperous lives.

We use the word, Spirit, to represent that Invisible Energy and Intelligence that brought forth the entire universe and most especially you and me. Spirit is present within you. Spirit speaks from the crown of your being as Divine ideas. The ideas are being made known to you 24 hours per day, 7 days a week. These Divine ideas come fully packed, clothed with every piece of information and guidance that you need to bring them into full manifestation. Your mission is to develop a consciousness of oneness with Spirit. Then, you will be increasingly aware of the absolute, total goodness that Spirit seeks to express through you. Like a baker who molds dough into delicious breads, pie crusts, cakes, and other delights, you will mold the divine energies into enterprises and ventures that bless you and the entire world.

How do you get started? Learn the Universal Principles that govern all of life and apply them to bless yourself and your world. The prospering results in the millions or billions will "Be added unto you." Reading the insights in this book is a great beginning. I know this because the Author is a "Johnnie Colemon Baby," who grew up in our church, _Christ Universal Temple_, based in Chicago. He is now blessing the world by making Universal Principles known to the world through the Internet, seminars, and publications. Dr. Cuttie Bacon, III, a retired educator, had labored for over a decade to bring forth a book on _teaching children to become millionaires_. After attending our basic course in Truth Principles, he was able to finish his book in a matter of months. Now, children and parents all over the world are benefiting from his spiritually sound, practical ideas. Les Brown, whom many know as 'Mr. Motivator,' was trained in our ministry and incorporates the Universal Principles in his lessons to millions on radio, TV, personal appearances, and the written word.

The Universal Principles are:

1. The Omnipresence of God.

Everything that exists or ever will exist is made out of the body of God, and comes forth in varying degrees of manifestation. Thus, every circumstance or thing that you meet in life is simply God energy waiting to be molded into some useful pattern for this world.

2. Divinity of Man.

Each individual on earth has divine spiritual capacities. You and all others around you can mold divine energies into useful patterns for the world. You and all around you can express the divine ideas of love, wisdom, power, life, and substance in your life fully.

3. Value and Power of Thought.

It is a truism that what "You think about you bring about." Watch your surroundings and yourself to see how efficient this truism can be. Change your pattern of thought and you change the pattern of events in your life.

4. Practicing the Presence.

When you are quiet enough long enough, you become aware of the high wisdom that is within you. Through your own method of prayer and meditation, you make contact with your inner Spirit that reveals the "orderly knowledge" you need to be blessed and to bless others.

5. Law of Demonstration.

What you are on the inside shows up on the outside. As you build your consciousness, your awareness, of Spirit's magnificent presence in you, you will be drenched in joy. This spiritual joy will serve as the magnet for attracting millions and more to you. But, the real prize will be the peace of mind and soul satisfaction that comes from working totally with God.

To know more about the principles, visit our website, *www.cutemple.org*. Remember, that I love you. Welcome to the world of the millionaire.

In His All-Prospering Name,

The Reverend Dr. Johnnie Colemon
Founder/Minister, *Christ Universal Temple*
Chicago, IL

CHAPTER 1

The Millionaire Motivator — Les Brown

"Among the easiest things I've ever done was to earn a million dollars; but the most difficult thing that I've ever had to overcome was to believe that it could happen to me. That's the real challenge. The bottom line when we start talking about wealth is there's a little known secret that most people never get. You don't get in life what you want; you get in life what you are, and that's why we must invest in ourselves"

— Les Brown

Born a twin in low-income Liberty City in Miami, Florida, Les and his twin brother, Wes were adopted when they were six weeks old by Mrs. Mamie Brown. Mrs. Brown was a single woman who had very little education or financial means, but had a very big heart. As a child, Les' lack of attention to schoolwork, his restless energy, and the failure of his teachers to recognize his true potential resulted in him being mislabeled as a slow learner. The label and the stigma stayed with him, damaging his self-esteem to such an extent that it took several years to overcome.

Les has had no formal education beyond high school, but with persistence and determination, he has initiated and continued a process of unending self-education, which has distinguished him as an authority on harnessing human potential. Les Brown's passion to learn and his hunger to realize greatness in himself and others helped him to achieve greatness. He rose from a hip-talking Morning DJ to Broadcast Manager; from Community Activist to Community Leader; from Political Commentator to three-term State

Legislator; and from a Banquet and Nightclub Emcee to premier Keynote Speaker.

In 1986, Les entered the public speaking arena on a full-time basis and formed his own company, Les Brown Enterprises, Inc. The company provides motivational audio/video materials, workshops, and personal/professional development programs aimed at individuals, companies, and organizations.

In 1989, Les Brown was the recipient of the National Speakers Association's highest honor: The Council of Peers Award of Excellence (CPAE). In addition, he was selected one of the World's Top Five Speakers for 1992 by Toastmasters International and recipient of the Golden Gavel Award.

In 1990, Les recorded his first in a series of speech presentations entitled "You Deserve", which was awarded a Chicago-area Emmy, and became the leading fundraising program of its kind for pledges to PBS stations nationwide.

Les Brown is also the author of the highly acclaimed and successful books, _Live Your Dreams_, and _It's Not Over Until You Win_. Les is the former host of The Les Brown Show, which was a nationally-syndicated daily television talk show that focused on solutions rather than problems.

Les Brown is one of the nation's leading authorities in understanding and stimulating human potential. Utilizing a powerful delivery and newly emerging insights Les' customized presentations are designed to teach, inspire, and channel an audience to new levels of achievement.

On Overcoming A Poverty Consciousness

"Among the easiest things I've ever done was to earn a million dollars; but the most difficult thing that I've ever had to overcome was to believe that it could happen to me. That's the real challenge. The bottom line when we start talking about wealth is there's a little known secret that most people never get. You don't get in life what you want; you get in life what you are, and that's why we must invest in ourselves. Many people want to change their lives and *change their circumstances, but they don't want to do the work to change themselves. Scripture says, 'Be ye not conformed to this world, be ye transformed by the renewing of your mind.' Most people will continue to live a life of poverty — not because they don't have the talents or the skills or ability, but most people are suffering from mental malnutrition. It's also because they cannot rise any higher than their thoughts and not willing to invest the time, energy and make the commitment to restructure their belief systems. Then, they will continue to manifest poverty in their lives although they have the capability of doing far more."*

On Reaching Your Potential

"People have far more potential than they realize, and consequently, because of social conditioning, circumstances and events in their lives, many people go to their graves ignorant to their true potential. Sometimes, we need to be reminded of what is in us. I like helping people to begin to see themselves differently and to ignite a different kind of thinking and behavior."

On His Millionaire Moment

"The first million I made was $1,600,069.10! I remember I made a million dollars in my mind before I earned it first. I was having lunch with someone that I didn't think had much talent, and this person made $13 million. After thinking about that for a while, I said, 'He can't be thirteen million times more intelligent than I am!' Then, I made up in my mind right there that I'm going to earn a million dollars over the next year."

On How Has Money Changed You And The People Around You

"Money doesn't really change you, money only makes you more of what you already are. If you are 'corn bread' like me, it just amplifies that. I ride in a limousine with the windows down because I paid too much for that car for you not to know that I'm in there [uproarious laughter]! You can take me out of the country, but you can't take the country out of me. I'm basically the same person that I was when I first started out. I'm still accessible and I still enjoy people."

On The Most Amount Of Money You've Been Paid For A Speaking Engagement

"I was paid $60,000 dollars once for two speeches because I charge $20,000 per speech and this company paid me $10,000 a day not to leave the hotel resort area to give the second speech. So, they paid me $20,000 extra just to wait; and I did! I was obedient!"

On Achieving A Larger Vision Of Yourself

"A person must achieve a larger vision of themselves beyond their circumstances, mental conditioning and the things that have happened to them. This begins to programmatically increase their sense of worthiness where they come to believe that they deserve more, decreasing their level of unconscious self doubt and self hatred that causes us to sabotage our future and work against ourselves. As long as we are stuck in justifying our victimizations, coming up with reasons and excuses of why we cannot move beyond where we are. Life has happened to everybody. That doesn't move us beyond where we are to where we want to go. There's an old saying, You can take a horse to water, but you can't make him drink. What you can do if you're skillful enough — you can create a thirst where they'll want to drink."

On Seeing Yourself In The Future

"Once you can see yourself in the future, then the associations with the people who are self-destructive or who could sabotage your future doesn't fit. The challenge with them is that they have a very limited vision of themselves. We're talking about creating a larger vision of themselves beyond the projects, beyond crack cocaine, beyond dropping out of school and having a house full of babies and not having a sense of worthiness, to creating a gang that will begin to have a larger vision of themselves, beyond getting pregnant and running around with drug dealers.

"People who see themselves in the future don't deal with people who deal with drugs. People who see themselves in the future begin to align themselves with people who see the value of education because they expect to be able to create the kind of future that they want. If you can't see yourself in the future, if you can't see how you

fit then you're going to act like a misfit. So, getting pregnant, being on welfare, blaming everybody for where you are, being a negative force to your environment comes naturally. As we begin to give them [young people] a larger vision of themselves and saying constantly that you have the power to live your dream, and exposing them to the messages that will begin to increase their sense of worthiness where they come to believe that 'Yes I deserve more; I can do this,' and decrease their level of self hatred that cause them to associate with other negative people, then our job is done. The message that I've developed is for the planet, regardless of who you are race, creed, color, age group, it doesn't matter. The language is universal. The method is applicable wherever you are."

On Feeling Deserving Of Having Wealth

"Because we have so much to overcome in our mental conditioning that many of the decisions we make and things that we do, we think it's us and really it's our preprogramming. Dr. Carter G. Woodson said, 'If you can determine what a man shall think, you'll never have to concern yourself with what he will do. If you can make him feel inferior, you'll never have to compel him to seek an inferior status; for he will seek it himself. And, if you can make him feel justly and outcast, you'll never have to order him to go to the back door, he will go without being told and if there is no door his very nature will demand one.' Overcoming the mental conditioning, that's the biggest thing — dismantling the lie."

On The Fear Of Failure

"One of the things we must understand is that you will fail your way to success. Walt Disney filed bankruptcy seven times and had two nervous breakdowns. JC Penney was committed to a mental institution with $12 million dollars in debt at age 56; but he died at age 92 with over two billion dollars because he did not give up. Once we begin to help people to overcome the fear of failure, I say make it okay that you failed. You're not going out to fail, but you will fail your way to success and all of those failures are learning experiences that will empower you — which means you are just one step away from success."

Philippe Matthews

On The Fear Of Success

"When you have a fear of success, you experience a feeling whereby you are not worthy, you are not confident and don't have the capacity to handle this. I've done that. I achieved something that I was very proud of and I ran because I didn't think I had the leadership and the capability to achieve and maintain it; so, I cowardly backed away from my dream and my own potential because I was afraid. You have to struggle with that fear, face it, embrace and move past it."

On The Importance Of Surrounding Yourself With People Who Believe That Wealth Is Possible

"It's very important because people rub off on you. You can go with one who wants to go rather than one who is around your neck. I'm reminded of John H. Johnson that said the first person he fired when he had this vision for Ebony Magazine was a very good friend of his. I asked him, 'Why did you fire him?' he said, 'I didn't believe that I could have this magazine, and I didn't believe in myself, so I didn't need anybody on my payroll to tell me that.' You've got to surround yourself with people who can see and reinforce your dream. One goose can fly 75% further in formation with other geese than it could ever fly by itself."

On Keeping Up With The Jones'

"I don't engage in that conversation. Achieving the goal is not as important as what you become in the process of pursuing the goal. The character-building skills, the knowledge, the wisdom, the confidence, the faith, the knowledge of being able to manage various tasks and being flexible, adaptable and realizing that you are either expandable or expendable."

On Teaching Kids About The Value Of Wealth

"What I teach is what scripture says, 'Money is thy defense.' Moreover, one of the things I teach kids is that being wealthy is your birthright. It is not the exception to the rule — it is a part of the norm. John Leslie [Les' son] started earning $2,500 an hour at age 15; so he will never be satisfied with a job. I teach that you can never get wealthy working for someone else. I teach kids to be

entrepreneurial. I teach my children how to earn money because a 'hand out' is a 'hand down.' I will teach them the character-building skills of what it takes to accumulate wealth and I told them to become wealthy not for the sake of wealth itself; but for who you have to become in order to do that. In order to do something you've never done, you've got to be someone you've never been."

On What Brings Les Joy

"Helping people to change their lives. I love people very much, and when I'm doing what I do...I love it. This gives me my life. If I go out like this, it will be fine."

For more information on Les Brown, visit his website :

www.lesbrown.com

Special YouTube Interview with *Les Brown on Being Parked*

CHAPTER 2

The Millionaire Maker: Brian Tracy

"If you have crystal clarity that your goal is to be worth a million dollars and that million dollars is clear to you then what you do is take the first opportunity that comes to you and move forward. You'll begin to attract in your life opportunities and possibilities."

— Brian Tracy

The average age of self-made millionaires in America is 55. It takes them 22 years from the time they get serious to the time they make it. Brian Tracy is one of America's leading authorities on millionaire development. He is a dynamic and entertaining speaker with a wonderful ability to inspire audiences to reach peak performance and high levels of achievement.

Originally from Canada, Brian started on his own road to success in his twenties when he left his home to travel across the world with a goal of crossing the Sahara Desert. He worked his way through Canada and the United States before securing a "working" passage on a freighter to England.

Currently, Brian is one of the top success experts in the world. He is an avid believer in controlling one's destiny, hard work and perseverance. He has trained two million people in 23 countries to achieve their financial goals faster than ever before.

His seminar, Make Your First Million, teaches participants to make more money, get out of debt, increase income and achieve financial independence. Brian explains, *"This is a seminar that is based on years and years of experience, including my own on how people become millionaires starting from nothing. It's a step-by-step process that helps people plan each stage of their lives, so that they can earn more money and double their income. I teach you several ways to double your income within the next 12 to 24 months. I show you how to deploy your funds and how to invest them to get the highest and safest return. I also show you how to protect yourself from using insurance, trusts, wills, family and limited partnerships, so that your money can't be taken by lawyers or adverse events."*

With a Bachelor's degree in Communications and an M.A., Brian speaks four languages, is extremely well read and regularly studies management, psychology, economics, metaphysics and history. Prior to founding Brian Tracy International, Brian was the Chief Operating Officer of a development company with $265 million in assets and $75 million in annual sales. He has had successful careers in sales and marketing, investments, real estate development and syndication, importation, distribution and management consulting. Brian has conducted high-level consulting assignments with several billion-dollar-plus corporations in strategic planning and organization development. Brian believes there are many facets to wealth building.

On Wealth Creating Activities

"I'm focusing on financial achievement and it's not based on buying dot com stocks. People ask me, 'How can I make money if the stock market is down?' and, I explain to them that a very small number of people make their money on the stock market. I teach about twenty-five different ways how people become millionaires and it has nothing to do with the stock market. People who are wealthy today park their money in the stock market after they have made it. People become wealthy by focusing on wealth-creating activities and trading stocks is not a wealth-creating activity—it's a wealth-deployment activity."

On The Importance Of Visualizing Self Employment

"There's an old saying that says, 'Success leaves tracks.' If you want to be successful, find out not only what other successful people do, but find out how other successful people think. We find that most

successful people see themselves as self-employed, which means they see themselves being in charge of their own lives and responsible for their own careers. This is a major shift that has taken place in the last decade. Today, no one is responsible for your career but yourself. The sooner you start seeing yourself responsible for your career, the sooner you'll start to make the kind of decisions that will assure you of a great career. If you keep waiting for someone to come along and take charge of your career, give you a job and give you the proper training, you'll wait forever."

On The 'Something For Nothing' Philosophy

"[There's a principle that I call] 'the something for nothing philosophy,' where everybody wants what they want as easily as possible. They want it at the lowest cost of time and money. That is a normal, natural, human construct. Geneticists will tell you the basic human physiology and anatomy hasn't changed in at least 25,000 years. We have the identical brain and cell structure of the first human remains. One of the constructs of human psychology is that we always seek to get the very most we can, at the very fastest and easiest way possible. Therefore, everybody wants to be financially independent. [It] is a natural human desire. You don't have to train people to want [it]. If I said to you that you could become successful if you worked hard for 20 years, or you could achieve the same level of success if you worked for ten years, which would you choose?

"You must realize that all successful money is long-term money. All real success requires a long process of personal/professional development of saving and handling money. One of the things I teach in Make Your First Million is the process of financial accumulation, which has never been taught anywhere. Most people don't know it and many of the books that are written on making money in the stock market are written by people who have only one narrow perspective on life and that's trading stocks. Trading stocks traditionally has accounted for a very small number of American-made millionaires. Most American millionaires come from people who either start their own business or who work with other growing businesses. Another industry is selling, five percent of self-made millionaires in America are sales people or people who specialize in a particular field."

On Self-Made Millions

There are many roads that lead to self-made millions and in America today, there are 7.2 million millionaires and of those, about 90% are self-made. There are approximately 300 billionaires, 80% of which are also self-made. Brian says, "That means they are first generation money. They started with nothing. Many of them were immigrants and came here with no language skills that are now worth hundreds of millions or billions of dollars. With all of these people making millions, there must be something going on here, so what you do if you're trying to replicate a process is find out what they did and you'll find over time, there are overlapping and repeating strategies and methods. And, what you do is identify the most common strategies and I've put them together in my courses."

"What I learned was that people who make their first million are not even aware of it! It's only many months later if someone does a financial statement on themselves, they find out they're worth more than a million dollars. I had to do a bank statement for a loan, I filled in all the blanks and added it up, and I was worth more than a million dollars and hadn't even realized it. That's how it happens with most people — they're so busy doing what they're doing that they don't pay attention to it. When you really pay attention to it — that's all you think about is your money, and you take your mind off your work. When you're focused on doing your job and doing it well, somehow the million dollars just appears on the radar screen."

On The Wisdom Of Creating Wealth

Before many dot coms went dot bomb, Brian discovered an interesting paradigm shift in the consciousness of the American people — people thought they could make a lot of money quickly. *"When a person makes a lot of money quickly; it gets into all of the newspapers like all of the dot comers and a psychological shift took place in the last five years. Before the 90's, people felt guilty about making a lot of money; however, from 1993 on, people felt guilty for not making a lot of money! In fact, people were a little angry that they weren't making a lot of money. It was a source of considerable exasperation for them. Now, we're going back to normal. There's one simple formula for becoming wealthy, and that is to add value and to keep some of it. The central focus of all wealthy people is adding value. How can you create a product or service that is of value to people and that is of greater value to them in terms of what they would pay than my entire cost to bring it to them? That is how people become wealthy; it's never been a secret."*

On Starting Empty-Handed

"I used to feel sorry for myself because I didn't have any money. Then, I found out later that nobody has any money and the story of American life is that everybody starts off with no money and what they do is go out and sell their own personal services. Everybody starts off with empty hands and the ability to work. If you get a good education, your ability to work is better than if you don't. However, if you have a college education, they found out that two years after you graduate from college, your education drops off like the first stage of a rocket — it's no longer important. All companies' today care about is can you do the job and do it well. That's why you have many young people who are real hard-chargers that are ending up ahead of older people."

On The Self Concept And The Laws Of Wealth Building

"In my estimation, it's the most important of all. They reason people don't earn a lot of money is because they don't see themselves capable of it. It never occurs to them that they can. You'll find that everything moves from the inside outward and when a person begins to say, 'I can be a millionaire, others have done and I can do it as well. I simply need to stay on track until I get there.' Once the people begin to conceive of themselves as capable of doing it, all sorts of things begin to happen. Then, the more things you do, the more you reinforce that self-concept and you begin to save your first $100; then your first $500; and first $1000; and when you begin to see it working, you move from wishing and hoping to positive knowing where you absolutely know that you're on the right track; and the interesting thing is that the more you stay on this track, the faster you move toward your goal and the faster it moves toward you."

On The 80/20 Rule

"There's a law of accelerating acceleration that I find is based on the 80/20 rule. The first 80% of the time that you work toward your goal, things will move very slowly. That is the testing time because that requires tremendous persistence. Suddenly, the last 20% of the time you work, you'll achieve 80% of your results. Therefore, the first 80% of your time you'll only achieve 20% of your results, and the last 20% you will achieve 80%. Most people quit during the first 80%, but if you keep working, it will work. A great example of this is franchising. The first branch of a successful company is not usually opened until the eleventh year. It takes that long for people to get a company to the point where they have the systems in place that are guaranteed for success before they can go across the street and open an identical business with the same system. The only way you can start a business and franchise is if it's a proven success system. For example, McDonald's has 30,000 outlets and not a single failure in its history — it's a guaranteed successor. So, if McDonald's comes along and opens up one of its outlets, they can tell you within one percent how much profit the owner will make each year."

On Direction

"If you have crystal clarity that your goal is to be worth a million dollars and that million dollars is clear to you then what you do is take the first opportunity that comes to you and move forward. You'll begin to attract in your life opportunities and possibilities. Almost everyone who achieves their financial goals achieves them in a totally different way than what they originally expected.

"It's quite remarkable when you start off in a particular direction and as you move in that direction, new opportunities open up to you that cause you to change direction and then as you move into that direction other opportunities open up which cause you to change direction again. As you keep following these opportunities, they lead you through the woods to your goals and when you turn around, you often find that you end up doing something completely different from what you had anticipated."

On Lessons Learned

"One of the biggest mistakes that I made was not being serious about financial saving and accumulation earlier. This is a big mistake that people make. They start off making very little, which everybody does, then they start to get very good at what they're doing or they get into a growing field where they make a lot of money and they think it's time for payback. They start to really enjoy this and start to spend money and they should be accumulating money but they feel they can do this any time. However, for now they want the bigger home and a nicer car.

"One of the things I would have done differently, is I would have been far more serious about saving ten, twenty percent of everything that I made irrespective of what was going on outside at an early age. Fortunately, it's worked out well for me because I realized that mistake. I realized I was on the wrong road and I started to become very serious about saving a few years ago and that's what changed my financial life. Everybody in life goes through hundreds of thousands and millions of dollars, the only question is, 'how much of it do you keep?' that becomes your true measure."

On Prosperity Guilt

"The primary reason for that are childhood experiences. It's a real tragedy but many young people are brought up by parents who made them feel guilty. If you're destructively criticized as a child, you grow up with deep down feeling of inadequacy and unworthiness so when you do begin to achieve some kind of financial success, you will feel unworthy. You will be struggling on the outside and contradicted on the inside where you actually engage in self-sabotage.

"Robin Williams once said that, 'cocaine is God's way of telling you that you're making too much money.' You'll find in the movie, 'Blow,' that all the money was made selling cocaine into the Hollywood community and the reason why is because many of these people are making more money than they ever dreamed of in their lives. They come from average backgrounds and very few from wealthy backgrounds who are successful in Hollywood. They start making money and feel overwhelmed because one of the reasons

that they're working so hard to be someone else as an actor is because they grew up with tremendous problems in dealing with themselves because of their parents. Therefore, they make all of this money and get all of these accolades and deep down inside they feel very conflicted so they self medicate with dope, alcohol, sexual promiscuity, and neurosis.

"Jennifer Lopez has a rule that when she appears, all of the staff is told to look at the ground when she passes. None of them are allowed to look at her face because she does not like people looking at her face — that is written into her contract. She does this because she is so far from her roots that they have not been able to adjust to it."

On Sense Of Self

"Arnold Schwarzenegger is one of the most respected persons in Hollywood and he had a very distinct life plan. He decided to become a millionaire before he went into acting and he did through bodybuilding and endorsements. Therefore, when he went into acting he was already a millionaire and he could actually select his roles. He's always been selective and he's never had this frustration or drive to be successful because he had success before he started acting. Therefore, he's always been very genial, and friendly. Everybody who knows him says the Arnold you see onscreen is the Arnold that you meet personally. He's very together.

"If a person doesn't have a very, very clear sense of themselves, then they will do all kinds of foolish things. The stories in Hollywood are perfect examples of people who stumbled into acting, did very well in a particular role and then become so confused about themselves that they made mistake after mistake after mistake. Many actors and actresses become very successful and they become so crazy that nobody will ever hire them again after making millions of dollars. Hollywood is a very tight community and they bet on proven talents or a demonstrative talent, which is someone that they know if they hire this person, they can depend on this person. They will come to the set, be prepared, they'll do the role, and they can invest the millions of dollars necessary to build this talent.

How to Make Millions When Thousands Have Been Laid Off

"A perfect example is <u>Alec Baldwin</u> *who was to be the leading man in all of the* <u>Tom Clancy</u> *movies. He had a good career and then he got cast in a role with* <u>Sean Connery</u> *for* <u>Hunt for Red October</u>. *In his contract, they stipulated that if the film were successful they would pay him a million dollars and his next film they would pay him four million dollars and negotiate subsequent movies. Therefore, Hunt for Red October was very successful and he came back and wanted four million dollars immediately. They said we have a contract where we only have to pay you two million for the second movie. Alec said, 'I don't care about the contract; you have to have me so you have to pay me what I want. I created that character and you can't make that movie without me so I want four million dollars — take it or leave it.' The studio said, 'thank you very much, we'll leave it.'*

"They hired <u>Harrison Ford</u> *and paid him six million dollars to do the movie and they took the Tom Clancy series around Harrison Ford and he now gets twelve to fifteen million dollars per movie and Alec Baldwin only gets walk-on roles and doesn't get anymore leading parts. Nobody will place him in starring roles because if you threaten one Hollywood studio, there's a gentleman's understanding that you won't work again. So, they spend all of their lives getting to the point where they have star quality then they turn on the very people who invested 80 million dollars in the movie to make them a star and they try to use extortion against them. It's because they are so far outside their self-concept, they are so far beyond anything that they ever dreamed of ever accomplishing that they can't adjust to it."*

On The Power Of Positive Thinking

"People are poor because they think poor. People become millionaires because they say, 'I always knew I'd be a millionaire.' Say that to yourself. Everything that is happening to me is part of a great plot, every setback I have is to teach me a valuable lesson that will help me become a millionaire. My job is to simply identify the lesson in each problem. If you have that attitude, you'll walk around like a learning machine. You'll learn from everything that happens to you. You get smarter and better all the time."

The Brian Tracy International Mission

We believe that everyone has a tremendous potential for development and growth, and that an investment in training is one of the most valuable investments a company or individual can make. Our commitment is to provide practical, results-oriented training and follow-up services to help individuals and organizations set and achieve their highest goals and aspirations.

For more information on Brian Tracy and his wealth of knowledge, seminars and products, visit *www.briantracy.com*

CHAPTER 3

Robert G. Allen: The Man, The Millionaire, The Difference Maker

"The source of all wealth is God. God knows where the gold is. You can't create wealth by yourself without having tapped into the source that knows what stocks are going up tomorrow, which pieces of real estate are going to be more valuable, which businesses have the best chance of success — you need to be tapped in. The way I do that is tithing."

— Robert G. Allen

As one of America's most influential real estate moguls, Robert G. Allen has shared his successful wealth-building techniques in popular seminars for the past 20 years in the United States and in every province in Canada. There are thousands of millionaires — representing billions in wealth — who attribute their success to his teachings.

Robert's philosophy and teachings are valuable because he's been through it all. Not only has he made scores of millions — but, on more than one occasion, has lost several millions as well. He is battle-tested, and proud of being from the school of hard knocks. Going through a bankruptcy was a humbling experience for Robert and his family. It caused him to look deep within to rediscover his values and purpose in life.

His infomercials are legendary and his best sellers have sold millions of copies. *Multiple Streams of Income*, *Multiple Streams of Internet Income*, *Creating Wealth* and *The One Minute Millionaire* shared his powerful money making systems. But, it was the New York Times #1 bestseller, _Nothing Down: A Proven Program That Shows You How To Buy Real Estate With Little or No Money Down_, that remains his signature book and serves as the all-time real estate investment classic used by beginning investors.

Robert is famous for following through on nationally publicized challenges. He once picked a couple out of a St. Louis unemployment line and, within a year of using his techniques, they had amassed over $100,000! He has hundreds of equally amazing documented stories to share. _"We did a challenge in May,"_ Robert recalls, _"where we wanted to make $24,000 in 24 hours. So, I called all of my experts and asked them if their life depended on it what would they do to make this happen. We came up with a process where we had 11,000 subscribers on our email list. On May 24, 2000 with the cameras rolling, we sent out a message that in one day, we offered some of the things that I do at ridiculously low prices, and when the day ended, we had turned this 11,516 subscribers into $95,532.44 in one day! That's when I got excited about the possibilities of the Internet. Before that time I hadn't used it that much. The average person spent about $900 on various seminars and private consultations."_

A resident of San Diego, California, Allen graduated with an MBA from Brigham Young University in 1974. Shortly thereafter, he began making small real estate investments that transformed his tiny nest egg into a large, multimillion dollar net worth in just a few short years.

On The Misconception Of Wealth Builders

"You've got half the population out there who think rich people are bad; then you have the other half that just don't understand. About 10% of the population is pure entrepreneurs. They like the concept of being their own boss. I literally cannot understand somebody who works for someone else and give their security away to some other corporate entity, I just can't comprehend that and they can't comprehend me. So, the misconception is the 90% that don't get what we do."

On The Accumulation Of Wealth With No Money Down

"Whenever I want to get involved in another business — it's got to be residual. If it's not residual, I don't want to play. It has to be something that doesn't cost a lot of money to get involved in. It's often said that the major reason that most businesses fail is under-funding or under-capitalization — that's a crock! What happens is, they end up borrowing money and invest in bad marketing. They run out of money because they are bad marketers. All the dot coms took their money and blew it on bad marketing. I would much rather start businesses on a shoestring, so I am forced to be smarter and careful with the way I spend my money. I think the chances of it being successful starting from a shoestring is much greater than a person who goes out and takes a second mortgage on their home and puts fifty thousand bucks in the bank, spends it all and blames it on the fact that they ran out of money. They would have been much better off if they hadn't have put their house up for a second mortgage and said, 'We're going to make this thing happen from day one!' It's got to be little or no money."

On Allen's Opposition To The "Think Big, Spend Big" Theory

"They have to have all the offices and employees — I'd rather have the right kind of business model so that you know it's scalable. However, the big dot coms thought they had to go out and burn several million dollars a month to try and take it to huge scale first and that's not smart."

On The Importance Of Marketing

"How you get a customer and keep that customer whether it's online or offline, it's the same thing. The difference with online marketing is that I get to fail fast for free. With offline marketing, you fail slowly for a lot of money! If I do a direct mail piece offline for 10,000 customers, it's going to cost me $5,000 minimum, two weeks to set it up and two weeks to get the results, I'm 30 days in to it and I've spent $5,000; and don't know if I made a dime. Whereas online, I send out 6,000 emails to our subscribers and 200 people bought my book through Amazon.com instantly, and it didn't cost me any money! Therefore, if I got zero response, it would not have cost me anything. However, the average person doesn't get that. If I tried to

mail 6,000 pieces of mail, it would have taken me a month, and I would not have gotten a 3% instantaneous return and response; so, Internet marketing is just on steroids!"

On The Six Wealth Resources

In his tape series, Multiple Streams of Income, Robert talks about the six wealth resources:

Mind

"You've got to fill your mind with information . . . Most people don't work on their brains. As soon as they leave school, they never read another book for the rest of their lives. 80% of people after they leave school never read another book, and only seven percent of the American population ever walk into a bookstore!"

Body

"When you exercise, you increase your stamina and you're able to put in more hours with more creativity with better, wiser decisions. My partner, Mark Victor Hansen, exercises daily. He's up at four or five o'clock every morning meditating then goes jogging or walks for an hour. Whenever we're traveling together, he calls me in the morning and says, 'Meet me in the lobby.'"

Being or Spirit

"The source of all wealth is God. God knows where the gold is. You can't create wealth by yourself without having tapped into the source that knows what stocks are going up tomorrow, which pieces of real estate are going to be more valuable, which businesses have the best chance of success — you need to be tapped in. The way I do that is tithing. Tithing is a principle that is usually not talked about very much because people get weird about it. It's not politically correct; but it's something that I've practiced my whole life. I've never met a really successful person that doesn't have a commitment to giving back. The difference is that you give back first instead of giving back last. When you give back last, you give what's left over, that's not how tithing works. It requires faith where you give your first fruits of the field. It's saying thank you for all of the blessings that I have, and that opens up possibilities that are just amazing."

Time

"You've got to be organized. Organization is the 80/20 rule. 20% of the things you do give you 80% of the results. For me, the difference between a poorly organized person and a well-organized person is the quality of their procrastination. A very disorganized person procrastinates the 20% and does the 80%. The very organized person, who gets the most done, does the 20% and procrastinates 80%. They both procrastinate. The secret to organizing is being a good procrastinator and most people are bad procrastinators — they procrastinate the wrong things. But, the most successful person on the planet is an incredible procrastinator — they put off all the things that really don't matter!"

"Don't do first things first, do feared things first. It will do two things for you. Number one, it will build your self-esteem because as you tackle a tough thing, you automatically build your personal self-esteem. As you put off that feared thing, it automatically lowers your self-esteem — it's the law of nature. The second thing is that you get such a buzz doing what you feared that it makes everything else pale by comparison and a piece of cake. If I do the easy things first, those are harder because in the back of my mind, I've got this gorilla I've got to tackle; which takes away all of the fun of doing the easy things. Somebody said you should start your day by digging a hole, throw in a bear and jump in!"

People

"It's time, task and the way you treat people. The most important person is who you are in the moment. The most important task is to do well and the most important time is now! So, whenever you're with somebody, remember they are the most important person and the task is to do them well and to do it right now — don't put it off. That's the philosophy I have with people."

Money

"Money is the spice of life. You don't have to have money to be rich, but you certainly can buy better memories. I believe a parent's task is to create good memories. Good parents create good memories, bad parents create bad memories — that's the bottom line. You don't

have to be rich to create good memories with your children — that's not a prerequisite, but it definitely helps. Money gives you the power to create more interesting and indelible memories. Money also creates lifetime satisfaction when you give it away in tithing. I don't buy this stuff when they say money doesn't buy happiness. Money does buy you happiness, but you can't get addicted to it. If you get addicted to money, it can cause you to forget people, God and your physical well being. But if you are in balance with money, it can be a very wonderful addition to your life."

On Wealth-Driven Guilt

"The Commandments say if you keep the Commandments, you will prosper. I use to feel guilty that I was building wealth and loving it. You should love God more than money. Put God first. That's why I pay my tithing first. When I was 35, I said to God, 'Thank you for the blessings, I'm a millionaire now and I want to do what you want me to do.' God told me, 'Why do you think you have all of this opportunity? You need to tell people how they can fix their financial lives.' This is my calling, this is what I'm suppose to be doing with my life, teaching people how to overcome the financial obstacles in their life and give them hope. Now, instead of feeling guilty for having money, I now feel guilty if I don't show others how to do what I've done. I love what I do and if you do what you love, you'll never have to work another day in your life."

For more information on Robert G. Allen, visit his website at:
www.multiplestreamsofincome.com
www.robertallen.com
Robert G. Allen on Nothing Down
Robert G. Allen on the Philippe Matthews Show

CHAPTER 4

Achieving Absolute Financial Freedom with Joseph J. Janiczek

"Financial Stagnation is a state of impaired action — when you are stuck in an inactive state due to some fear, conflict or mental block. If you look at the United States, you are talking about 90% or more of the people suffering from some form of financial stagnation. The biggest difference between multimillionaires and the rest of us is that they have learned the cures of financial stagnation — how to act consistently in the face of adversity. Master the cures to financial stagnation and you end up on the fast track to abundance."

— Joseph Janiczek

"Never Worry About Money Again!" are the profound words that come from the lips of Joseph J. Janiczek, a noted Denver-based financial advisor with the highest credentials in the financial advisory profession (Masters Degree in Financial Planning and Chartered Financial Consultant Designation) and author of the award winning book: *How to Achieve Absolute Financial Freedom*.

I personally was struck by the comprehensiveness of his book and literally use it as my personal financial planning and wealth-building bible. A 440-page book he wrote that stems from his philosophy that everyone can achieve financial freedom. Joseph explained, *"Most of these concepts were developed over a ten-year period in the giant laboratory of my practice."*

I think that's what makes the book unique — all of these concepts were developed in the trenches with individuals struggling with money and trying to master money. "I have over 700 one-on-one sessions per year with individuals." Joseph says it was a personal journey as well as a business journey that created this mammoth financial diary. *"I was brought up in Chicago with very modest means but always desired financial freedom and I was always fascinated with the opportunity and freedom to build a business. I started with absolutely nothing and worked my way up to owning many businesses and having a substantial income and net worth where I absolutely do not worry about money and have not for many years now; and in the process I built a financial advisory practice dedicated to helping many others do the same."*

Joseph has a vast amount of practical and academic experience specifically in the area of personal finance. He has the highest level of education in the financial advisory profession (Masters Degree in Financial Planning) and also has Graduate Certificates of Specialty in Investment Management and Income & Estate Tax Planning. Mr. Janiczek also has the highest undergraduate certification in the financial planning profession, which is the Chartered Financial Consultant Designation. He has been recognized as one of the "100 Great Financial Planners" by Mutual Funds Magazine and his book: *How to Achieve Absolute Financial Freedom* (*www.AbsoluteFinancialFreedom.com*) was awarded a Gold Medal as the Best Business Finance Book of the Year and a Silver Medal as the Best Overall Design by CIPA in 2001.

On Financial Dysfunction

"Common dysfunctional beliefs that cause problems are: 1) Being in a constant "Distrust" state about the financial markets — it brings on fear and inaction, the two most common causes of bad investment mistakes. 2) Not making peace with the past — it causes us to live in the present with resentment and look to the future with resignation. By making peace with the past, we look to the future with ambition — a critical ingredient to success. 3) Entitlement — when we feel entitled to something we stay in a state of frustration and disappointment because we feel we no longer have the power to

control our lives. This is devastating to the achievement of absolute financial freedom.

"Common bad habits are: 1) Bad debt habits — abusing credit cards and personal loans. I believe in the philosophy of no such debt, regardless of interest rate. 2) Bad spending habits — living above or equal to our means with little awareness or control. Doing so reduces our standard of living in the future, particularly when we stop earning income. 3) Bad saving habits — being addicted to immediate gratification and never setting aside funds for our long-term needs. To put the powerful force of compounding in our favor we need to consistently save first."

On Financial Stagnation

"Financial Stagnation is a state of impaired action — when you are stuck in an inactive state due to some fear, conflict or mental block. If you look at the United States, you are talking about 90% or more of the people suffering from some form of financial stagnation. The biggest difference between multimillionaires and the rest of us is that they have learned the cures of financial stagnation — how to act consistently in the face of adversity. Master the cures to financial stagnation and you end up on the fast track to abundance."

On The Stretch Zone

"There are three 'zones' we live in from day to day that determine whether our circle of influence is growing or shrinking: The financial comfort zone, the financial stretch zone and the financial panic zone. If we stay in our financial comfort zone (continuing to do what we always have, and which we feel most comfortable) our influence in the world shrinks. If we learn to continually thrive in the financial stretch zone (where we feel mild to medium resistance but take new actions and learn new things) we consistently grow our influence. Far outside the stretch zone is the financial panic zone (which represents actions way out of our comfort zone) which are actions that might be favorable to you, but incur so much resistance that it is difficult to maintain for a consistent amount of time. What I have found is that being in the stretch or panic zone can both produce results, but for better results, I recommend consistently taking action in the stretch zone. The stretch zone enables small

steps of progress on a consistent basis rather than giant dramatic steps on an inconsistent basis; just like the drips of water that started the creation of the Grand Canyon, consistency always prevails!"

On The Difference Between Stretch Zone And Panic Zone

"Let's say you had someone who was into saving money in CDs their whole life and suddenly they're not happy with the 3-4% return, so they go and seek to invest in stocks (an action outside of their comfort zone). One option is to jump in and buy whatever has been hot — like an Internet Stock back in the late 90's. Another option is to dollar-cost-average (adding a little each month on a consistent basis) into a diversified, balanced mutual fund. Jumping in by buying the Internet stock is jumping into the panic zone, and a bad week where the stock drops 10% or more is all that would be needed for this investor to jump back into the comfort zone by selling, taking a loss and vowing to never look at anything outside of CD's again. Conversely, selecting the option of consistently investing into a balanced mutual fund would likely produce long-term desirable results. The investor would build confidence as they endured up and down and sideways markets, realizing that they significantly outperformed the CD over five years or so. The stretch zone builds confidence to stretch even more; this is why it leads to success."

On Making Mistakes

"The idea is to grow and to take action. However, to take action, you are going to make mistakes from time to time and you can have your greatest learning experiences by making mistakes like most of us do. If we are brought up thinking that mistakes are bad, we basically put ourselves in financial stagnation because we don't take action. Whereas, if we are brought up living in the stretch zone and making mistakes from time to time, which is a natural part of success, we find that we can actually learn from mistakes and grow, that's where real growth happens. When I look back in my life, the greatest mistakes I made is where I've had the greatest breakthroughs. We don't usually recognize it in the middle while we're going through it, but when it changes our behavior and helps

us see life at a different level and we learn from it that is when we make great strides forward. So, don't handcuff yourself by thinking mistakes are bad."

On Learning To Learn Again

"The greatest competitive advantage anyone could ever have is the ability to learn and to learn faster than others. The idea of learning to learn again is that there are many things that stop us from learning, and we get into ruts. What's ironic about learning is that we tend to get into a state of "blindness" about learning as we master a topic. Blindness is when you don't know what you don't know. Oftentimes, when someone becomes an expert, they suddenly think that they know it all, and that's when blindness stops their progress. The idea is to get to a state of "ignorance" where you know what you don't know; so you can learn again. Schools and society has pressured us all into thinking we need to be a "knower" all the time in order to be successful. Whereas, those who are innovators and grow are constantly in a state of learning, they don't feel like they know it all; they feel they know only a small fraction of what is available. It doesn't mean that their confidence is low, or they think badly of themselves. Contrary to popular belief, they are constantly searching to learn and it's that posture that is so important to the achievement of financial freedom, as well as any other success in life."

On The Enemies Of Learning

"The enemies of learning are automatic responses (habits) that shut off the opportunity to learn. 'I already know this,' 'I don't need to know this,' 'this is boring,' and 'this is not fun,' are examples of the enemies of learning that need to be identified and eliminated. Think back on a problem that you were confronted with today. Did you use any of the enemies of learning to 'write-off' the problem? As you become aware of this problem you can learn to disrupt the pattern and learn in the face of resistance. Our environment constantly challenges us with opportunities to grow and learn. Being in a constant state ready to turn a challenge, problem, success or mistake into a learning experience enables us to continually expand

our circle of influence and results. I call this a key seed of financial freedom."

On Habits By Design & Habits By Default

"You can change your life to be anything you want it to be by changing your habits. Habits are powerful forces in your life that represent the combination of actions and behaviors you execute on a conscious and subconscious basis daily. We all have habits in every domain of our life and we are 100% disciplined to them. It is enormously powerful to recognize that we have habits by default and habits by design, and successful living is all about choosing and changing our habits to be aligned with our goals and values. Habits by default are those that we developed over time from the influence of our parents and world without much thought — they can be empowering or disabling. When it comes to money, a common habit by default is spending everything we earn. This habit often got its root when we started out in our careers, earning a small amount and spending every dime to make ends meet. The problem is when we allow this habit to continue, even when our income begins to increase. If you now make a high income but still don't save, this spending habit by default is the cause.

"Now, a habit by design is a habit you purposefully master. I believe that one of the most powerful things anyone can do is to specifically and deliberately identify what habits they want to master and then act until they have mastered each new habit by design. For example, a powerful financial habit by design is to save 15% of your net income off the top no matter what. In my book, I have identified the dozen or so Habits of Financial Freedom that result in the achievement of absolute financial freedom. These are shortcuts to success because they are already identified and refined. It took me 20 years to pinpoint these powerful habits. Master them, and you master money."

On Habit Germination

"I say it takes 40 months to master a complex habit (like mastering money), and forty days to master a single habit (like saving money). The key is to focus in on one habit by design at a time until completed — when it goes on autopilot. The key is to devote prime

time to habit development, not left-over time. For instance, when you identify the habit you want to master, do something that demonstrates your mastery of it the first thing in the morning (wake up early if you need to) rather than when you have the last ounce of energy at the end of the day. You will be tested over and over until you master the habit, so keeping focused and determined is the key to your success. Once you have learned to master habits by design that are aligned with your long-term goals and values, life and the world becomes an exciting menu of opportunities for you."

On Financial Mentors

"Financial mentors have been a very powerful influence in my life. I highly recommend that everyone be on the lookout for people who have been successful in achieving things that are similar to our own long-term goals and values. Be very discriminating in your selection, as they will have a powerful influence in your life. Interview them, ask them questions and learn from their successes and failures. I think it is important to find mentors who motivate us, and who we highly respect."

On Progress Vs. Perfection

"It is very important to have long-term goals that are essentially ideals that we continually strive to achieve. The problem is when we constantly compare our current results to a far off ideal, and it constantly puts us in a state of frustration that hinders progress. I think it is much more effective to focus on the progress we are making from day to day, how we have progressed from the last week for instance, and celebrate the progress. This gives us a sense of accomplishment and confidence that enables us to take action to achieve the next bit of progress toward our ideal.

"I maintain a success journal that identifies what accomplishments I have made and why they are important to me. I then identify the follow-up and precise first steps to build upon such success. This is a powerful weekly habit that increases my productivity tremendously. It also keeps me in good spirits and at a high state of confidence, particularly during challenging times — when I need the encouragement the most. Do this same action every week and

you will find that you are able to be much more productive and confident."

On The Process Of Financial Freedom

"There are many sound strategies that are absolutely bulletproof. Many people are on a destructive course without knowing it. They are at risk of depleting their assets. For example, inflation and taxation, not to mention spending, will erode the largest of portfolios over time. The very best advice I can give someone today is to put time, spending, rate of return, and tax deferral/exemption on their side. This means taking action today to optimize their finances from an investment, income taxation and estate taxation perspective."

On The Two Biggest Mistakes People Make

"The biggest mistake is waiting until later. Most people don't realize is that they spend the rarest of all resources and the most critical element to financial compounding foolishly: TIME.

"The second biggest mistake is a lack of critical success information. What people DON'T KNOW costs them thousands of dollars in needless penalties and lost income. Considering that the financial livelihood of our loved-ones and selves are at stake, both mistakes should be avoided at all costs. Mortality tables show we are living much longer than before. In most cases, the widow has to bear the brunt of poor financial and investment planning."

On The Top Three Recommendations From How to Achieve Absolute Financial Freedom

1. Raise your financial standards. When we identify what we will and will no-longer stand for, we evoke powerful forces in our lives. Thus, getting in a fed-up state and saying: "I will no longer tolerate credit card debt," or "I will no longer tolerate poor investment results," or "I will no longer tolerate not having an updated estate plan" is a powerful Seed of Financial Freedom.™ Raising your standards is therefore a powerful first step towards achieving absolute financial freedom.

2. Develop your financial habits. What we do on a consistent basis has more of an influence on our lives than any other factor. It is not the economy, stock market or anything else. To harness this power, identify and act on the habits that result in absolute financial freedom. It has been my life's work to identify the shortest list of habits that result in absolute financial freedom. Habits like the saving habit, debt habit and investment optimization habit. Make it your goal to identify what habits will improve your finances the most and immediately begin mastering them. The most comprehensive part of my book identifies the Habits of Financial Freedom, a powerful list of habits that I believe result in absolute financial freedom.

3. Focus on Progress rather than Perfection. Many people make the mistake of thinking that they have to figure it all out before they begin — this stops them from acting. Rather, focus on the progress you are making and your confidence will grow to take even more action and make more progress into the future. How to Achieve Absolute Financial Freedom helps people focus on progress rather than perfectionism, clearing the way for great growth.

Joseph J. Janiczek's Top Three Always List

Always put financial compounding in your favor by putting time, spending, rate-of-return and tax deferral/exemption on your side.

Always put the power of consistent action in your favor. Success comes from good judgment. Good judgment comes from experience. Experience comes from taking consistent action.

Always have a written asset allocation plan, written financial freedom plan and a written estate plan. Your assets and income will grow more consistently, retain more of their value and you'll achieve more of your objectives. The bottom-line is that you will sleep much better because you will be on the path to achieving absolute financial freedom.

To obtain more information about The Absolute Financial Freedom Program contact Janiczek & Company, Ltd. at 303-721-7000.

www.janiczek.com

CHAPTER 5

Bob Proctor: The Mentor to Millions of Millionaires

"Faith is the ability to see the invisible, to believe in the incredible and that will permit you to receive what the masses call impossible."

— Bob Proctor

Bob Proctor is an author, lecturer, counselor, business consultant, entrepreneur, and teacher preaching the gospel of positive thinking, self-motivation and maximizing human potential. In that endeavor, he follows in the footsteps of such motivational giants as *Napoleon Hill*, *Earl Nightingale* and *Wallace D. Wattles*. But Proctor carries the message of these great teachers a step higher and explains them in terms understood by tots and tycoons alike how a person goes about recognizing their potential and how to apply this effort in setting and achieving life goals.

Bob Proctor's insight is rooted in the fact that he lived an aimless, purposeless existence for the first 26 years of his own life. Born in a little town in northern Ontario, Canada with the low self-esteem that often befalls the middle child. He performed poorly in school, dropped out and joined the Navy. After his term, he drifted aimlessly from one dead-end job to another until a friend recognized unrealized potential in Bob. The friend introduced Bob to the concept of self-development through Napoleon Hill's classic *Think and Grow Rich*.

With the spark generated by Hill's words, Proctor found the initiative to start an office cleaning business, which he grew to international scope in his first year of operation. From that experience — after seeing what he had been able to accomplish with a mere rudimentary knowledge of personal motivation and goal setting — he hungered for more information. His quest took him to the Nightingale-Conant organization where he utilized every opportunity to study under his mentor, Earl Nightingale. His intense study earned him an invitation to join the organization where once on board, he rose swiftly through the ranks. Moreover, while the Nightingale-Conant organization assumed the forefront in wide-scale distribution of personal development programs, Bob decided to take his ideas and methods directly to the individual, on the one-on-one level.

In the mid 1970's, Bob established his own seminar company and secured a contract to work with a few hundred agents of Prudential Life Insurance Company of America in Chicago. During his first seminar Bob made the lofty declaration that any determined agent could write $5 million in business during that calendar year. He was met with skepticism. How was that possible? The seminar took place in July with the year half over. No agent in that region had ever written so much business in the 100-year history of the company. Nonetheless, they agreed to try. When the performance level of the entire division increased substantially with more than one agent actually accomplishing what was previously unattainable, Bob's reputation as a motivator was established. For several years since, Bob has shared his special message and expertise with hundreds of corporations worldwide and through a program of live seminars with thousands of individuals of all ages in all walks of life. Bob Proctor's speeches and lectures are memorable, packed with the information, inspiration and wisdom to transform the lives of his audience members.

Meanwhile, in addition to his international bestseller You Were Born Rich, he found time to author other works as well, including *Mission in Commission*, *The Winner's Image, The Goal Achiever*, *The Secret*, *The Success Puzzle*, *The Recruiting Puzzle*, and Being Your Very Best. Unlike many programs, which convince you that you can do anything you set out to do, Bob Proctor's programs complete the cycle by explaining what you must do, why you must do it and, more importantly, how it should be done.

On Genetic Conditioning

"I think we're programmed. I think it's for a lot of reasons that we believe a lot of other nonsense. It's genetic and environmental programming. People don't think and live with what they are programmed to believe. Moreover, there's so many poor people around that it would seem to make sense — they can't all be bad people. I think we're conditioned genetically. It's not an accident that you look exactly like your uncle Harry. The genetic conditioning is very strong and on top of that you have environmental conditioning. Unfortunately, we're programmed to take everything and reverse it. It's like we live from the physical to the spiritual when we should be going from the spiritual to the physical. We live through our senses. If you go by your senses, you're going by the appearance of things and the truth is very rarely in the appearance of things."

On Being Born Rich

"We've got deep reservoirs of talent and abilities within us. There's so much power locked up in us and it's never used. We're rich in resources — everyone is, most people are just a little short of money but riches the most erudite scientist alive won't guess at what you and I are capable of doing."

On Knowing How Much Is Enough

"Well it depends on what you're doing. To accumulate money just for the sake of accumulating money is a fool's game and you will usually end up pretty unhappy, probably a sick person. Money is an instrument and it's used for two things. One is to make you comfortable and the other is to extend the service that you offer beyond your own presence. You'll hear people say, I really don't want money, I just want to do good, well Wattles [Wallace D. Wattles] pointed out many years ago if that's the case you should get rich first because the good you can do without the money is limited to your own presence. So money is an instrument that enables you to extend what you're doing far beyond where you are."

Philippe Matthews

On Money And The Decision To Make It

"It is a wonderful servant but makes an absolutely terrible master. Money will do whatever you tell it to do. It's greatly misunderstood. Almost everything we've been taught about money is false. Money has nothing to do with race, religion, gender, geography, it has nothing to do with formal education, it has nothing to do with your background, and it has nothing to do with your intelligence. There are some very intelligent people who are broke and there are people who are not very bright at all who are multimillionaires! Money is based on one thing, decision. You decide you're going to have it or you decide that you're not."

On Being Led By Faith

"Where people get hung up on goals is that they're trying to figure out how it's going to happen before they set the goal and anyone who has ever accomplished anything of any consequence has never known how it's going to happen. I always point out that 'how' is God's job and 'what' is your job. You decide what you want done, and God does the work with and through you. Clarence Smith is a man who I haven't seen for years but he's a brilliant guy who I asked what was faith to him and he said, 'faith is the ability to see the invisible, to believe in the incredible and that will permit you to receive what the masses call impossible.'The ability to see the invisible, there's a power flowing into your consciousness and you have creative faculties in your consciousness that enables you to build an image of anything you want — anything, no limits! No one can alter it, no one can shorten it, and no one can change it. You have the ability to picture anything you want — to see the invisible — you see it before its moved into form. To believe in the incredible. Its incredible to believe that there's a power that's resident in every cell of your being and when you take that image and mentally let it move into the subjective form of your mind, that part of you will instantly and automatically alter the vibratory rate of your body, change your behavior and change what you attract into your world. It will manifest the image you hold in physical form. Its an absolute law!"

On The Importance Of Thinking

"Well, we don't think. We don't see it because we're trained to see just through our eyes. I remember spending five years working with Earl Nightingale many years ago and he said, 'if more people said what they were thinking they would be speechless.' When you hear that it sounds pretty funny, but if you think about it, it's true. Most people mistake mental activity with thinking but it's not. They're going to old movies and if you stand back objectively and observe peoples behavior, it's obvious that they're not thinking or they never would do what they doing. On the other hand, if you listen to their conversation, it's obvious that they are not thinking or they would never say what they're saying. I think it was the late and great doctor Ken McFarland that said, 'two percent of the people think. Three percent think they think and ninety five percent would rather die than think.' Thinking is the highest function we're capable of and if you want to do something and you think about how you can, the way will be shown."

On Mental Reflexes

"Many of our decisions are made purely on the mental reflexes we've built up through similar decisions made hundreds of times over the years. In fact, we spend a great deal of our lives on autopilot."

On Vision

"It has to be service oriented because wealth is a reward received for service rendered. You have to have an image of doing something that's extraordinary and I think everyone wants to. I believe we're spiritual beings and the essence of the human is spirit and spirit is always for fuller expansion and expression. That means there's something within you that wants to express itself in a greater way and that will keep you wanting more than what you got, wanting to do more — jump higher, run faster, make it bigger and It's not to have it or to do it, it's to create the awareness that you can. You have to have a vision of what you want. Most people compromise, they're not going after what they want at all, they're going after what they think they can do. Going after what you think you can do

is never going to inspire you so you'll probably quit. We should ask ourselves 'what do I want?' and throw away all of the limits. It doesn't matter what it costs, what help you're going to need or what's required — just what do you want. When you decide on what you want and you take that in your mind, you will attract everything that is required for the manifestation of that image."

On The Difference Between Wants And Needs

"I think a person should look after their needs because if they don't take care of their needs, they're going to have a very difficult time focusing on their wants. However, taking care of our needs is such a puny, little thing to do — anybody can take care of their needs. If a person is not thinking, they may have difficulty. There was a time when I didn't think and I had a difficult time taking care of my needs but as soon as I began to think, I never had a difficult time taking care of my needs and I've always gotten what I wanted."

On Expectation

"That goes back to the conditioning again and the conditioning controls the vibration you're in. The vibration dictates what you will attract. When we start to understand our relationship with Spirit or with God and how our mind functions then it's easy to start to expect great things to happen because you know what the creative process is. When you really understand the creative process, expectation is a natural thing. Expectation is a mindset that controls the vibration you're in and that controls what you attract into your life. Expectation is more of an intellectual thing and faith is more of a subjective thing. Faith comes from understanding. Faith is an emotional thing — it has more to do with the subjective mind. Expectation without faith is useless — it's wishing. It's the understanding that gives us the faith. With knowledge, you wouldn't need any faith. This is really paradoxical because the more knowledge you have the more faith you have and the more knowledge you have the less faith you need. It's a real paradox."

On Individuals Who Have No Exposure To Wealth And Possibilities

"I do believe a person can be born into dire circumstances and there are certainly a number of them. I think Spirit is resident there and it's omnipresent. I think spirit is pushing at their consciousness to do this. If they let the old paradigm control them, they won't do it; but, every now and then you'll see a person come out of the ghetto or out of a very bad situation and they follow that impulse from inside and they step out and things start to happen and they do it. I also believe that you and I have a responsibility to try and reach out and wake those people up. That's what I spend my life doing."

For more information on Bob Proctor, visit his website at:

www.bobproctor.com

CHAPTER 6

The Culture Shock of Rich Dad, Poor Dad: Robert Kiyosaki

"Most people want to have what the rich have but, the way they do things is try and work hard and it's really hard to work hard and get rich. You have to be rich mentally, emotionally and spiritually. You have to say, 'It doesn't make a difference what I do — I am a rich man and I will be a rich man.' You've got to come from a being — body, mind and spirit of a rich person. So, it doesn't really matter what you do."

— Robert Kiyosaki

Born and raised in Hawaii, Robert Kiyosaki is a fourth-generation Japanese American. He comes from a prominent family of educators. His father was the head of education for the State of Hawaii.

After high school, Robert was educated in New York. Upon graduation, he joined the U.S. Marine Corps and went to Vietnam as an officer and a helicopter gunship pilot.

Returning from war, Robert went to work for the Xerox Corporation and in 1977 started a company that brought to market the first nylon and Velcro "surfer" wallets, which grew into a mega-million dollar worldwide product. In 1985, Robert founded an international education company that taught business and investing to tens of thousands of students throughout the world.

Retiring at the age of 47, Robert continued with his love of investing. It was during his "retirement," he wrote *Rich Dad Poor Dad*, the #1 New York Times bestseller. Robert followed with *Rich Dad's Cashflow Quadrant* and *Rich Dad's Guide to Investing* — all 3 books have been on the top 10 best-seller lists simultaneously on The Wall Street Journal, USA Today and New York Times.

Concerned about the growing gap between the "haves" and "have nots" Robert created the patented board game entitled, "*CASHFLOW® 101*," which teaches individuals the same financial strategies his rich dad spent years teaching him the same financial strategies that allowed Robert to retire at the age of 47.

Rich Dad Poor Dad reveals what the rich teach their kids about money that the poor and middle class do not. "The main reason people struggle financially," Robert says, "Is because they spent years in school but learned nothing about money. The result is people learn to work for money but never learn how to have money work for them."

Robert's rich dad taught him about the four distinct differences between the people who represent these letters in the Cashflow Quadrant. E stands for Employee, S means Self-Employed or Small Business. B stands for Business or Big Business and the I stands for Investor. After reading about the differences and the language between these four mindsets, you'll be hard pressed not to categorize everyone you meet in these four groups.

For instance, the E mentality will always talk about how they need a secure job and a steady paycheck but they always seem to complain about their financial status — never making enough, always wanting more, but not willing to take a sensible step toward true financial freedom vs. financial security

Although Robert's business is real estate and building businesses, his true passion in teaching. He is a highly acclaimed speaker on financial education and his work has inspired audiences worldwide. His commitment to teaching people how to become rich is even offered to the E's and S's that work for his companies.

On Ways To Get Rich

"There are many ways you can get rich. One of the most popular ways is by being cheap. My rich dad once told me that you can get rich by being cheap but the problem is that once you are rich you're still cheap! You know people like that, they're just as poor as if they were poor but they have all of this money. What they've done is make money their God. The other way you can get rich is you can marry somebody for money — we know what we call people who do that. It's a popular pastime! Another way you can get rich is inherit it; but we all know by the time you're fifteen if you're going to inherit anything or not. And, another way you can get rich is by being a crook. You can get rich, but you're still a crook and the trouble with being a crook is you really have to be a smart one because if you make a silly mistake, you're talking about five to ten years in jail. The ones who will sue you are in the crook category because they have justified in their mind that they can steal from you. That's why you want to incorporate and have good attorneys around you, have good insurance and things like that. The last way you can get rich is by being generous. If you look at the richest people on earth they have really been generous at some level. For example, McDonald's sells billions of hamburgers and Microsoft sells an operating system."

On The E Mentality

"It's shocking! It's called Emotional Intelligence. What I found out is that the emotions are twenty-five times stronger than thought. So, if you have a rattlesnake in front of you, you're afraid of it, and someone says, 'Don't worry, I've taken the fangs out and it's harmless,' you're still scared because it's a rattlesnake. Most people look at money, they see a rattlesnake sitting there, and they're terrified.

"Their fear is greater than logic. It's like when you see a good looking woman and you know she's going to hurt you; but, it's worth it! You know she's going to break your heart but you get involved anyway. Think about this, as soon as you see a woman that you don't want, you don't care if she shoots you down, but if the woman looks like Julia Roberts, you already know she's going to shoot you down. Your emotions form your reality. But, if you think you're Brad

Pitt, you'll go and talk to Julia Roberts. However, if you're Robert Kiyosaki, you might hide at the end of the bar. You see, in my mind, I've already lost the game. So, if you say, 'I'll never be rich,' that's the power of emotion."

On Early Retirement

"Statistics show that you give up all of your wealth in the last year of your life because your hospital bills gets you. The average woman whose husband dies, goes through all of her husband's net worth in less than two months. Those are national statistics and that's because people are so afraid that they would rather play it safe and pretend that everything is going to be all right and remain the same in the future. Well, it's not. You've got to start thinking about retirement earlier. I started thinking about it when I was about 15, because my poor dad kept telling me to get a secure and safe job and that I could retire at age 65. I said to myself, 'Why would I want to do that?' I want to retire early so I can get on with my life! So, I planned to retire when I was 35 and it took me until I was 47; nonetheless, I made it out. I lost a couple of times, but I learned to make money without working — do you know how priceless that is? Do you know what it's like getting up every morning and not know what to do? I set my life up so that I could retire early and have all the money I wanted."

On Developing A Financial System

"There are three basic types of financial systems or assets, one of them is a business. The second is real estate. For example, if I buy a house and rent it out to someone else. The third is paper assets, which are stocks, bonds and mutual funds. These are all systems that are assets. I spent my life acquiring those rather than looking for job security."

On Wealth And Tax Laws

"I had to do it. I bought [a Ferrari] so that I could get my tax rates down." In his CD series, Rich Dad Poor Dad, Robert explains that there are only two types of money problems, not enough money or too much money. *"My Accountant called me up and said, 'You don't have a car.' I say, 'Yea, I know, I paid for it.' She goes, 'Stupid! You*

need some debt, you're making too much money.' So, I went and leased a Ferrari, just so I could get the payments up . . . There are three kinds of tax laws — poor, middle class and rich. Unfortunately, the schools don't tell us that."

On Making The Transition From An E And S To A B or an I

"To make the transition from an ES to a BI; first of all, it's your attitude — then, you have to have a plan. You can do it as an employee but the trouble with an employee is that 50% of your income is taxed and you can't do anything about it. Whereas with me, 35% of my income is taxed, but I can at least control it by deducting like crazy whereas an E can't do that. All of my cars, phone bills and when I travel — all of that is pre-taxed expenses. Whereas if I'm an employee, it's an after tax expense, so the laws are different."

On Employees And Financial Security

"Their job is to make me rich and my job is to make them rich. All I can do is share with them the information that I have. All of the people who started working around me have started their own companies — I encourage it. They don't leave because they know I'm looking out for their best interest and real financial need — not just giving them a pay raise. For instance, the woman who cleans my house, recently bought a franchise. My bookkeeper, she finally went out and bought twelve properties and she's financially set. See, if you like your work and you're getting rich, you'll stay but if you hate your work, you'll leave. My Director of Marketing is only 28 years old and I told him to form his own real estate investment company, and he said to me whether I pay him or not he's going to get rich; so, I teach people how to take control of their life. The more I encourage my staff to become financially free, the happier they get at work. The people that work for me know they're not going to get rich working for me; but they come to our courses and I'm always teaching them how they can find what works best for them. I want them to become financially free."

On Getting Rich At Home

"My rich dad always said that 'You don't get rich at work, you get rich at home. If you look at Michael Dell, he started Dell Computers in his dorm room. You look at Hewlett Packard; it was started in a garage. My wife and I started this business on our kitchen table. It's really hard to get rich at work because the laws are not in your favor."

On Financial Intelligence

"Money doesn't' make you rich. Money has the power to make you rich or poor. If you look at most NFL players 65% are bankrupt after three years of leaving the NFL, but they make a lot of money. Look at lottery winners; most of them lose their money. Money doesn't make you rich, financial intelligence makes you rich while the lack of it makes you poor."

On Not Working For Money

"I work to acquire assets and my assets make the money for me. I work hard to build a company, or to buy real estate or play the stock market but I don't want to work for that money, my assets work for that money."

On Recognizing True Assets

"Most people want to argue with me that their house is an asset and I tell them that if you're paying for it, it's a liability. They say that their house goes up in value, but I tell them 'yes, but today, you're paying for it and if you don't pay for it they'll take it from you so that's a liability.' I've got a friend who rents taxicabs to immigrants. He rents them out so that his taxis are assets. He's the B; or the Business Owner, and the guy driving the cab is the S; or Self-Employed."

On Having No Personal Assets

"I don't want to own anything personally, and if I do, I've got to watch out because someone may sue me for it. That's why you want to look like you're deeply in debt because if you get sued it looks like you're an idiot. Let's say that I have a $100,000 house and I have no

debt on it and someone goes to an ambulance-chasing Attorney and they see that I have a $100,000 house free and clear and the attorney will come after me. But, if a $100,000 house has $99,000 in debt, he's not going to come after me because I have no money. So, you have to know when to look rich and when to look poor. There are two people that always want to take your money, one is the government and two, people who want to sue you — it's a fact of life. When people find out you have money, they'll come after you."

On Being, Doing, And Having

"Most people want to have what the rich have. But, the way they do things is try and work hard and it's really hard to work hard and get rich. You have to be rich mentally, emotionally and spiritually. You have to say, 'It doesn't make a difference what I do — I am a rich man and I will be a rich man.'You've got to come from a being — body, mind and spirit of a rich person. So, it doesn't really matter what you do. For instance, I'm a teacher but I make millions, and millions of dollars teaching because I come from, in my opinion, a rich being-ness. I don't do much but I have what millionaires have. People who do not understand that you have to be wealth before you know what to do to have wealth also feel as if there is not enough money to go around and how can they have a piece of the pie.

"That is a programmed thing but, it's absolutely not true. The thing that my rich dad told to me is that the older you get, you should get healthier, you should get happier, you should become more in love and you should become richer. Because that's the way God set everything up. The trouble is that our school system uses Malthusian economics. Thomas Malt wasn't an economist, he was a protestant preacher and his belief was that economics is the study of the allocation of scarce resources. So, the assumption is that there is scarcity. But, if you look at it, there's so much more money today that the Fed is printing it up like crazy. Everyday, 2 trillion dollars trade hands and you're not getting any; something is wrong with that! Once you snap into the mindset and skillset, the possibility is staggering."

On Attitudes Of The Wealthy

"For me, the biggest thing is self-criticism and laziness. I'm from Hawaii! But, you have to be very smart to be lazy. It's like the story of Tom Sawyer where they paint his fence, well, Tom may be lazy but, he's smart. Those people who were painting his fence are hard working and what most people are, are the people who are painting the fence. If you want to be rich you have to be lazy but smart. My rich dad use to tell me the key to success is laziness and incompetence. If you want to be rich, then the less you do — the more you make. What happens to people is that if you think you have to get rich by working hard like the S's and the E's, you will work hard. What I say is that the key to success is laziness. I'd rather buy an asset that's making me $100 a month — well that's $1200 a year that I don't have to work hard to make. When I write a book, I write it once and I sell five million copies, whereas there are reporters who write every single day but they never get rich and they're better writers than me. So, the key to success is laziness, but smart laziness."

On Belief And Trust

"My friend once said that everyone wants to go to heaven, but nobody wants to die! But, what has to die is your ego. I go out and do something and if it's the right thing to do and it's in spiritual laws, then it will work. However, if it's the wrong thing it won't work and I've done a lot of things that don't work but it doesn't' stop me from doing the next thing. That's why I've only had a job for four years of my life. Because I trust that if I'm doing what I'm supposed to be doing, God will take care of me. I wrote my book not because I had to make money, but because I knew I had to do it. If I didn't do it, I would die and I knew it. I sat in 1994 on a mountaintop in Southern Arizona and asked the question to God, 'why do I feel like crap?' The reason was is that my job and my work wasn't over yet. He said to me you have to go do this and I said, 'Oh shit; I hate writing, I can't write books.' But, I wrote it anyway and created the game [Cashflow 101], and now I'm rich again."

On His Guiding Principle

"With every dollar in your hand, you have the power to choose to be rich, poor or middle class."

For more information on Robert Kiyosaki, visit his website at:
www.richdad.com
Full Video Interview of Robert Kiyosaki on the *Philippe Matthews Show*

CHAPTER 7

Teaching Kids How to Be Millionaires: Dr. Cuttie W. Bacon, III

"Large conglomerates are being bought out and are downsizing at a rate that children of the future that do not know how to run their own business may end up broke. So, starting a home-based business is the first lesson on how to really make money in this country."

— *Dr. Cuttie Bacon III*

Dr. Cuttie Bacon III is the epitome of understated wealth. Classy and confident, it was a long journey toward financial independence for the Bacon family. Born in Western Kentucky, Dr. Bacon lived the first four years of his life on a farm where his Father was a farmer. He grew up in Louisville, Kentucky, finished high school and graduated from Kentucky State University. He moved to Chicago where he earned a Master's Degree at Loyola University in Chicago, and a PhD at Northwestern University in Evanston, Illinois.

Dr. Bacon has taught at Northwestern University, Mundelein College, Governors State University, and National College and has led numerous seminars over the past 20 years. His administrative experience in Education started as a Principal and later as a Superintendent of Schools in the Southern Suburbs of Chicago, where he began seeing the need to teach children how to manage money and how simple it is to become a millionaire. Not only should his book, *How To Teach Kids to be Millionaires,* be read by children, it should be read by parents as well. In his book, Dr. Bacon explains why a child or parent should save $1-2 per day, which will reap the benefits of financial power later.

Cuttie Bacon frequently speaks on "How to Live a Rich and Prosperous Life" and numerous other educational topics. Cuttie recently published his second work: _How to Write and Publish Your Own Book._ Cuttie is an entertaining speaker and is able to see the humorous side of life in any subject and is known for his workshops and speeches on classroom management and administering an effective school.

On Saving Money

"It's important to save one to two dollars a day for your child because one, it's a model experience. You are modeling for the child what he or she should do with money. Most parents know how to give a child a dollar or two a day, and let them spend it on useless things like candy, gum and junk. When you constantly do that for twelve years, children grow up believing that a dollar or two has little or no value and the only possible thing to do with it is to race to the drugstore and spend it. Giving a kid the practice of spending two dollars a day for 365 days a year, you show them exactly how to throw away $600 a year. In ten years, they've thrown away $6000. If you invest in a mutual fund for the child at 15%, they may very well have $7000 in twelve years. That's the lesson that you want to give the kid.

"It's difficult and complex because the basic rules of growing money have not been taught to youngsters, young adults and older adults. Nobody in this country that has limited financial education believes that a dollar or two a day over 40 years will add up to a half a million dollars! The reason being is we do not teach them about compound interest. Compound interest is taught at elite schools and for people who already know what compound interest already is. When you grow up in a family with a trust fund at 12 years old; you are very clear that $100,000 in your trust fund is going to be $1,000,000 when you turn 21 years of age. For example, the Kennedy's and the Rockefeller's knew that, but if you grow up in a house with a $50,000 a year income, your parents don't know, your grandparents don't know so, they understand that to make you happy, is to give you one or four dollars a day to spend. But, if they don't know that same dollar can grow into thousands of dollars, they can't depart that kind of information onto their child."

On Saving With A Low Income

"Families with incomes of $1,000 to $20,000 a year believe that they are locked in poverty, and that they will be locked in poverty for the rest of their lives. When they get a dollar or two, they think the reasonable way to gratification is go to a fast food place, spend it quick and enjoy it. That's their level of enjoying four or five dollars because they have no notion of how money grows. Most people who were born in this country were not born into money, and become wealthy by investing a dollar or two a day. They did not become wealthy in this country because they had thousands of dollars to invest."

On Saving Versus Investing

"The major difference between saving money and investing money is that I believe that saving money is the first step toward investing. Nevertheless, someone who saves for 20 years works like this. The average savings account will bring you 5%. If you put 100 to 300 dollars a year into a savings account, you will find out how quickly it will double by dividing 5 into 72 — it's called Financial Rule 72. 5 into 72 goes 14 times. Therefore, it would take that $300 dollars 14 years to double. Conversely, if you divide 15 into 72, you will find that it goes less than five times so, in 4.5 years, your $300 will double compared to 15 years.

"I always ask people, 'Would you rather have your money double in four or five years than fourteen or fifteen?' So, if you have $300 invested in this year, four or five years from now, you will have $600. Nine years from now, it would be $1200 and fourteen years from now, it would be $2400. If you invested in a savings account at 5%, fifteen years from now, you would have $600; so, you have 4 times as much money if you invest it in Mutual Funds. In stock, it could be even better. For example, back in the 60's, I invested a small amount of $5,000 in Abbott Labs, which was very strenuous for me to do at that time. However, that same $5,000 in 1992 was worth a million dollars! So, with your savings account, save until you get $1,000 in the account; then invest it in Mutual Funds and stock. Saving is not where you want your money to go, investing is when you want to double your money."

Philippe Matthews

On Saving Versus Spending

"How you spend money really determines what kind of money you are going to have. One of the things that I learned researching millionaires is they have a habit of not spending a lot of money. They spend a small percentage of their earned income and most of them can tell you where every dollar goes. They save money because they don't spend it. For example, one who can give an account for every dollar spent every day for thirty days can tell you where every dollar went, and they can also look at their spending practices and see where they can save more money the next month. The person who does not keep a record and an account of their spending, has no idea what they can save and they truly believe that they need to spend every penny that they get — whether they make $50,000 a year or $150,000 a year! In the book, *The Millionaire Next Door*, one of the constant events that are mentioned throughout the book is that millionaires are very frugal people. They do know how to handle a dollar and the reason why they are millionaires is that they have learned how to keep the money and save it rather than spend it."

On The "Poor Rich"

"Many people who have $250,000 income have things like $10,000 mortgages a month, it is not uncommon for them to have two $75,000, $100,000 luxury cars that will give them a $2-3,000 car note. Additionally, it is not uncommon that they eat at the finest places, they dress in the finest designer clothes and they spend 125% of their income. You see, spending that much of your income never allows you to accumulate anything in terms of investments, because it takes everything to cover your month-to-month expenses, and each year you get another $20,000 in the red, which leads to what we've had in the last two or three years in this country — the highest domestic bankruptcies in the history of this country, along with the highest credit card debt."

On Allowance Versus Wages

"I think the way you teach kids about money should be related to real-life experiences. In our adult lives, nobody gives us money for anything. Nobody walks up to us and says, 'You get so much money

every week for breathing.' In life, you earn it. You either invest it or work everyday, or have a business — you earn your money. Now, if we're teaching kids to get ready to function as adults, we should not have any false experiences. Every experience should be an educational and learning experience, which that means that if a child is going to receive $10 a week, he has to earn it the same way an adult does. A job or a service has to be related to it, and the child has to be required to work and be paid for that. If he does half of the work, he doesn't get $10, he gets $5. If we go to work two and a half days a week, we get paid for two and a half days a week — we don't get paid for five. So, each one of the experiences with money as it relates to children; I think, has to be related to real-life experiences. Because, the child does not grow up believing that somebody is supposed to give them money.

"I taught my children that I was not going to give them money. Because I brought them up believing that I was suppose to give them money, they would come and ask for loans or gifts of $500 or $600 — whatever they thought they needed. So, I had to re-educate them at 25 years old, for example, my kids would say, 'Dad is not giving away anymore money — so, don't ask!' My last financial gift to them in life was giving them a down payment for their home, and they were not to ask for another penny! I had my children prepare and sign a document, which stated, 'Dad gave me a down payment on my house, he's not going to be giving me or lend me anymore money in my life!'"

On Teaching Children To Be Entrepreneurs

"I had the fortunate or unfortunate experience at ten years old telling my father that everybody in the neighborhood was getting an allowance, and I wanted to know when I was going to receive one. He said, 'Never. Your allowance will start when you get a job or business.' I said to him, at ten years old, 'I'm too small for a job or a business.' He said, 'I beg your pardon, you may not be able to get hired, but I'm going to show you how you can earn your allowance.' Therefore, he built me a wagon and put 'Delivery Boy' on it, and I would have to knock on every door for three blocks, telling the neighbors that I could go to the store for them and deliver their goods back to them with my wagon. Then, after I made $3 one

Saturday, my dad said, 'You now have your allowance.' He shook my hand and congratulated me and said, 'How much money do you have?' I said, 'Nothing.' He said, 'What did you make Saturday?' I said, '$3.00.' He said, 'What did you do with it?' I said, 'I spent it.'

He said, 'I forgot to tell you one thing — never spend all of your money. Bring me 25 cents out of every dollar and give the rest to your mother. So, from now on if you make three dollars, give your mother 75 cents to put up for you and save and before you spend your money, check with your mother and see if she needs anything — she may need to borrow from you!'

"Home-based businesses are one way of really teaching a child how the American economy works. This country is made up of huge amounts of small businesses. We do not have a thousand General Motors or IBM's, we have thousands of small businesses. And, it's this huge conglomerate of small businesses that we can use to teach our children how to earn a living and earn money in the future. We have to teach them this because the large conglomerates are being bought out and are downsizing at a rate that children of the future that do not know how to run their own business may end up broke. So, starting a home-based business is the first lesson on how to really make money in this country."

On Types Of Home-Based Business For Kids

"Last week I interviewed 25, African-American children between the ages of 9 and 14, who are all CEOs of their business. One had a Balloon Delivery Business. He delivered balloons for anniversaries, parties, standing on the street corner — selling them and in school. One had a Cookie-Making Business. She made cookies, gift wrapped them and sold them all over town. Another had a wonderful Shoe Shine Business. For example, he went to five high-rise buildings that contained 100 people in each building. Then on Saturday's, Sunday's and evenings, he and his brothers would make their appointments and usually, a guy would bring out five pair of shoes and they would shine them for $2 apiece. They told me they net $500 a month part-time.

"As you know, two months after a kid gets a new toy, he throws it aside because television would tell him there's another toy out. Well, this one brother and sister — for two to five dollars, would buy discarded toys and take them in other communities where kids don't throw them away, doubles the price and sells them. Some of the toys are brand new with the price tag attached, and they have a toy-recycling business. There are huge numbers of businesses; candyman businesses are very big in neighborhoods. Therefore, any business that can be housed under the roof of your house, parents can teach their kids how to earn a profit. One of the most famous home-based businesses was a toothpaste business. There's a young man in Cleveland, Ohio called, The Toothpaste Millionaire. Over twenty years ago, his grandmother showed him how to make toothpaste with baking soda before it got popular with the bigger companies. Between the ages of 12 and 14, he was able to start a small shop with the help of two adults; he was able to clear more than 1 million dollars in toothpaste sales in Cleveland, Ohio. He has a book out called, <u>The Toothpaste Millionaire</u> *— [about] a kid who started a home-based business that got so big that they turned it into a regular business while he was in the eighth grade, and made a million dollars in one year. So, it can be done."*

On Self-Employment

"You're the best boss you'll ever have. You're the only boss that won't fire you. You're the only boss that really knows how much vacation time you need! How long you need to sleep and how much you need to eat and spend. You should be the one to make all of those decisions. Being self-employed and owning your own business, you can make all of those decisions. It's very hard in the larger companies to become CEO. You can appoint yourself as CEO in your company before you ever make one dollar!"

On Teaching And Timing

"The first time to start teaching kids about money is the first time they ask for a nickel, dime, quarter or dollar. When a child asks you for money, trust me, they know what they're asking for. They do not expect for you to give them candy, they do not expect for you to give them food. When they ask for money, they are talking about paper

money, and at that point, it is time to let them know that money doesn't grow on trees and to get money, you have to give a service or earn it. Budgeting time should follow close behind that. As soon as you give a child a dollar, you should let them know that this is the first and last time that you are going to do it, or the child should tell you what he or she is going to buy. Then, you tell them to buy half of that and the other 50% is going into his or her piggy bank — that is the first lesson in budgeting. That lesson should be graduated with every dollar they touch. If their grandmother gives them $10, they should never be able to spend $10. Five of that should go into a piggy bank and five should go on school supplies. Those are the early lessons in budgeting that are absolutely necessary for the child to be financially secure as an adult."

To order Dr. Cuttie Bacon's books, call (800) 955-9934 or email him at: *cuttie3@compuserve.com*

BONUS CHAPTER

Lessons in Leadership, Stedman Graham

"Cultivating leadership qualities is really an investment in self. It's about leading, managing and controlling yourself in such a way that other people see your example and aspire to where you're going. Leadership is about a vision and being able to have a vision greater than yourself and the people who want to follow you. That can include your family, your friends, and co-workers. Particularly in corporate America, where people follow you because you are a visionary. They're not there just because the money is good; they are there because of the vision that you have. They want to go in the same direction; so they follow you."

— Stedman Graham on Leadership

Thirty minutes from Atlantic City lived a family of six children in an all Black town with a population of 1200. In Whitesboro, New Jersey, Stedman Graham fought with self-doubt and low self-esteem, but ironically, grew up to become one of the world's most inspirational leaders and an authority on the subject. Stedman Graham is Chairman and CEO of S. Graham & Associates; an Educational Company that creates customized corporate training and leadership development programs.

At 6' 6", Stedman's presence not only captivates a room, but so does his message. He has completely transformed himself into an advocate of leadership development with best-selling books: <u>You Can Make It Happen</u>, <u>Teens Can Make It Happen</u> and <u>Build Your Own Life Brand</u>. Although he's the head of several companies and community organizations, it wasn't easy.

His father was a painter, and mother was a housewife — always looking for a way out of the mediocre mindset he was living in. Stedman explains, *"I always wanted to excel because I grew up with a race-based consciousness, and I believed that I was less than because of the color of my skin. So, I grew up with that kind of stigma and victim mentality. However, basketball and sports was a way out. Sports were a big thing in our town because everybody played sports; therefore, I wanted to be a good baseball player, basketball and whatever else I played. That was really my way out because I didn't understand the meaning of the word 'education', and I didn't understand the full value of education. So, sports were the outlet and all of my role models at that time were in sports. For example, Wally Jones and Lou Jackson, Wilt Chamberlain and some of the older guys that were prominent in that era."*

Determined to succeed, Stedman held strong in his vision of creating a new self-image. *"I was trying to fill that hole in my heart; trying to feel that I was as good as everybody. I grew up with low self-esteem and a lack of confidence in myself; so, I didn't know how the process worked. I didn't know how to be exactly who I wanted to be. You can dream about it, talk about it and maybe even visualize it, but as far as putting the mechanics in there, I really didn't have that information."*

Stedman received a Bachelor's Degree in Social Work from Hardin Simmons University and earned a Master's Degree in Education from Ball State University. He has been awarded an honorary Doctorate in Humanities from Coker College, and has been recognized by the American Advertising Federation as an Industry Influential for his work in support of diversity.

Though he has clearly accomplished many milestones, Stedman says his self-development is still an ongoing process. Stedman's professional development has been guided by his nine-step empowerment philosophy, which is detailed in *You Can Make It Happen: A Nine- Step Plan for Success,* and is designed to manage both professional and personal situations.

A commitment to education and lifelong learning is central to Stedman's philosophy. He is an Adjunct Professor at The Kellogg Graduate School of Management at Northwestern University, where he developed and teaches the first sports marketing curriculum for second-year MBA students. He also co-teaches a Kellogg Management and Strategy course entitled, Dynamics of Leadership. In addition, Stedman is a distinguished Visiting Professor at Coker College, and a Visiting Professor at The George Washington University (GWU), as well as a Founder and Former Director of GWU's Forum for Sport and Event Management and Marketing, which was the first of its kind in the country.

Equally crucial to Stedman's philosophy is a commitment to youth and community. He is the Founder of The Leadership Institute of Chicago, a nonprofit education and research organization dedicated to promoting effective leadership throughout society. Activities include seminars, programs and lectures, philanthropic activities, publications, and primary research. Stedman is also Founder and Executive Director of Athletes Against Drugs (AAD), a nonprofit organization of athletes and other civic leaders committed to developing leadership in youth. AAD provides in-class curriculum to Chicago Public Schools and conducts corporate leadership visits, parent workshops, role model presentations, community and volunteer projects, as well as sports clinics with professional athletes. The AAD College PREP Program helps high school student-athletes secure college scholarships.

Additionally, Stedman serves on several charitable boards of directors including the National Board of Junior Achievement (JA). He initiated and directed the creation of JA's BASE Program (Building Achievement through Sports and Entertainment). BASE is comprised of curricula and activities to introduce middle and high school students to the business aspects of sports and entertainment.

On Leadership Qualities

"Vision, I think is the biggest quality; then trust, and then believing in yourself and having the confidence, so that you have the ability to communicate effectively where you're going and how you're going to get there. I also think it's having the experience and people

wanting to follow folks that understand what they're doing and have been there before. Then, have the courage to keep going when times are tough."

On Vision And Complacency

"You have to have some unique qualities that will allow you to have exposure. You must have a vision of yourself that sets you apart from the average person and leaders are not average people — they don't go along with the status quo — they step outside of the box, which is what makes them unique. Therefore, being able to have the experience, exposure and being in the mindset where you want to create even more value for yourself as a person. Most people are very comfortable with their lives and do the same things over and over again every single day, so they don't really expand themselves. Leadership is really about expanding, experiencing and creating opportunity based on extending yourself and not putting yourself in a comfortable situation."

On His Mission

"I'm still a work in progress. What I like is the experiences that I've had that have set the example of doing something that other people can benefit from. I try to work as much as I can in an area that will help other people and share information that will help other folks. My leadership is about empowering other people — that's my mission. I would like to be exposed to as many people as possible that share the message and give them the right information so they have the ability to lead themselves."

On Taking Care Of Oneself

"In the course of my day, I try to get up about 5:30 a.m. and be in the gym at 6:00 a.m. I remember hearing Mrs. [Coretta Scott] King in one of our leadership classes' talk about how Dr. King had to be in shape. He had to watch what he ate and had to have enough energy based on the schedule that he had. A lot of times we forget about what it takes to be able to have such a grueling schedule like Dr. King had and she mentioned that you have to take care of your body. I think health is a big piece in determining how much you're going to get done in leadership. The other thing I do is have a vision

for myself. I understand where I'm going and how I'm going to get there. I'm able to put together a schedule months and years ahead that allows me to create projects that really support the overall vision of where I want to go."

On Self-Esteem And Change

"I think that it has been very difficult for me because of the way I viewed myself and the way that I thought about myself. When you grow up trying to find yourself — having low self-esteem, lack of confidence, and you don't understand the process, you don't have the tools to be able to withstand the pressures of anything. However, when you begin getting the tools and understand clearly more of who you are, that becomes a confidence builder for yourself — you don't give external things power like you use to."

On self-Discovery

"[It's really important to discover] who you are and what your passion is. That really is the foundation piece for development. Unless you have that foundation and identity, it's very difficult to go to the next step, which is vision. It's hard to develop a vision for yourself if you don't understand who you are in terms of leadership. Conversely, if you can't clarify who you are, where you're going and how you are going to get there, it's very difficult to lead because you don't have clarification of who you are. How can you help me when you don't have yourself together in terms of where you want to go?"

On Stepping Into The Outer Limits

"Overcoming your fears is learned so when you go back and look at your family life — check your ID, see how you were programmed in life. What were you told to do, and reevaluate that programming if that's applicable to the way you're living today? Oftentimes, what you learned from your parent's years ago is not even applicable to the world you currently live in. So, you have to constantly reevaluate the present based on the messages of the past. Continue to reassess your programming and take control of your life, and you will begin to develop your own program based on your own human potential, which is the greatest gift in the world."

On Winning By A Decision

"Somebody spent a lot of money on research so they can get the right information to make the right decision, and oftentimes, we make decisions at the drop of a hat without really getting the right information. How many times have you made decisions based on somebody else's information that may be wrong? So, win by a decision is about making good choices in your life and that determines what your life is going to be like."

On Making An Effort And Getting Started

"It takes a long time to try and figure out who you are — it's a lifelong journey, but you have to start somewhere. I talk to people all over the country and too many people never even start. They never begin because they are so wrapped up in their schedule and being programmed to do the same things over and over again. They never really think about themselves and always think about what's outside of them. If you never go inside to discover what you really want to do, you waste a lot of years giving everything away."

On The Investment To Be A Leader

"You have to look within yourself and develop an investment within yourself and the work you do on yourself is directly related to the relationships that you build outside of yourself. The idea is the better you are and the more internal capacity you can build for yourself, the better relationships you will have. The better relationships you have, the better opportunities you'll have to share and learn. The more you learn, the more options you have. The more options you have, the more wealth you'll have. And, the more you have, the more you have to give."

For more information on Stedman Graham, contact S. Graham & Associates at:

www.stedmangraham.com

Stedman Graham | Entrepreneurial Panel Discussion

ACKNOWLEDGMENTS

I would like to thank God for the many days that I woke up and didn't know what to do, where to turn and how I would make it through.

God has carried me this far by faith and I only wish to continue being His servant to help the men, women and children who may have lost their hope and dreams somewhere along the road toward self-discovery of life.

I would like to thank the Reverend Doctor Johnnie Colemon, of Christ Universal Temple in Chicago for being my Mentor, Role Model and Spiritual Leader since I was 10 years old. It was your principles and teaching ministry that led me through all of my victories, valleys and massive successes.

To my Mother, whom *I made three promises* to before she died in my arms when I was 14 years old.

I would also like to acknowledge my Sister, who took care of me after our mother and father died. You looked beyond my faults and took care of my needs — I am forever grateful for your courage and belief in your baby brother.

To Dr. Cuttie Bacon, III, who truly believed in my dream and raised my level of thinking with every conversation and meeting. It was also Dr. Bacon who showed me how to be kind rather than be right.

To Sifu Tony Roberts, for being a second Father, and all my brothers and sisters in the Dojo for giving me discipline, courage and the wisdom of many generations.

Philippe Matthews

To all of the phenomenal mentors and self-made millionaires featured in this book who shared their dreams, knowledge and possibilities with me that has forever changed my life and future.

A special thanks to Les Brown and Brian Tracy, my role models in the introduction to personal and professional growth. Les is like the Father I wish I had, and Brian is the Uncle whose wisdom will last an eternity.

To Bob Proctor, who took me under his wing and offered unconditional love, support and has become a family member!

God bless all of you for reading this book, applying the powerful wisdom shared in this book and for the faith you have in yourself to become a proactive force in your life.

Finally, this book was first authored by me in 2001 and is dedicated to the families and individuals lost during the World Trade Center and Pentagon Tragedy, on September 11, 2001; and for those individuals who courageously gave their time and efforts in helping healing America. These individuals, both past and present, truly represent the spirit, strength and compassion of America, and will not be forgotten.

ABOUT THE AUTHOR

(Extended Biography - The Oprah of Internet)

Philippe Matthews is the Executive Director of the *HOWmovement.org*, a 501c3 dedicated to teaching people HOW to MOVE from the illusion of Hope to the Process of how and reveal the potential for success that resides in every man and woman. He is also an Internet Marketing Technologist and CEO of *MyInternetMarketingExpert.net*; an SEO and Social Media Marketing firm near San Francisco.

Philippe is best known as the host of the Philippe Matthews Radio, TV and Blog Show, which has over 750,000 collective listeners, viewers and readers worldwide! As a result of the success of the Philippe Matthews Best Internet TV Show, Philippe Matthews has been touted as the "*Oprah of Internet*" by co-author of Chicken Soup for the Soul, Mark Victor Hansen.

The Philippe Matthews Internet TV Show produces, daily, weekly and monthly content in blog, video and internet radio format and offers advice from world class thought leaders, the best how to advice, self help, interviews, profiles, experts, and authors on the topics of money & finance, personal, professional and spiritual development, beauty and style, love, sex & relationships, technology profiles and reviews and more!

If you Like "O"; You're Gonna Love "P"

Offering a forum for provocative, intelligent and uplifting dialog, Philippe Matthews says, "*I don't ask questions that are different; I ask questions that make a difference.*"

Philippe Matthews

Because of Philippe's unique Internet Marketing, SEO and Social Media Marketing experience, the Philippe Matthews Show offers a unique marketing advantage and platform for guests and sponsors of the show. When guests and sponsors come on the show, they receive a powerful SEO, Internet Marketing and SMM campaign that promotes their brand, product and/or service 24/7 through multiple internet channels such as online video, blogging, internet radio and social media.

Philippe has profiled such business leaders and experts as Michael Gerber, Stedman Graham, members of Donald Trump's Season One of The Apprentice, Kristi Frank, Heidi Bressler, and Jessie Conners. Financial experts such as Suze Orman, Robert Kiyosaki, Sherrin Ross Ingram, Natalie Pace, Ryan Mack, Kim Kiyosaki, Sharon Lechter, Dr. Penelope Tzougros and Paul C. Wright. Spiritual leaders such as Deepak Chopra, Marianne Williamson, Carolyn Myss, Iyanla Vanzant, Michael Beckwith, Rev. Dr. Johnnie Colemon, and Wayne Dyer.

Personal growth and development experts such as Les Brown, Zig Ziglar, Susan Taylor, Dr. Denis Waitley, Bob Proctor, Dr. John F. Demartini and Chad Stewart, Dr. Brian King, Dr. Louanne Brizendine, John Bradshaw. Technology and social experts, Marc Ostrofsky, Eric Hamilton, Tammy Fennell, and Animesh Tripathi.

Global icons and entertainers such as Russell Simmons, Denise Matthews, Jimmy Jam and Terry Lewis. Beauty and style experts such as Suzanne Somers and supermodel Beverly Johnson. Health and fitness experts such as Lou Ferrigno, Frank Zane, Lee Labrada, Lenda Murray, Sharon Bruneau and Carla Dunlap.

The Journey

From poverty to prosperity, Philippe Matthews is a native of Chicago, Illinois whose parents divorced by the time he was age 6. By the time Philippe was 10 years old, his mother was told by doctors that she only had three to four months to live. Philippe dropped out of school to take care of his ailing mother while his older sister worked to support the family.

Philippe's mother began reading an inspirational journal called the "Daily Word" and found a church near their home that his family began attending during their mother's illness. The church was Christ Universal Temple, headed by the Reverend Doctor Johnnie Colemon and Philippe mother lived another four years versus four months!

One night while taking a shower, Philippe heard his sister screaming. He rushed out only to find his mother gasping for air. As he held her in his arms praying, she took her last breath and made her transition. At that moment, Philippe made three promises to his mother, "1) I will never get involved in gang activity, 2) I will never do drugs, and 3) I will make something of my life that you would be proud of."

Their phone and lights had been disconnected so Philippe had to ask a neighbor to call an ambulance to retrieve his mother and to ask if he could call his father and tell him what happened. His father, a plumber, who he had not seen since he was 6 years old, came back into Philippe's life at a pivotal time but only after two months of having his father back in his life, one day after helping his father work, his father got out of his car and literally dropped dead while Philippe helplessly watched.

Devastated, Philippe called his sister and told her the news and his long journey of self discovery began. Despite the dire and stressful circumstances of his life, Philippe made good on the promises he made to his mother and did not allow himself to fall prey to the pitfalls of the environment that ensnared so many of his peers.

Instead, he forged ahead through life constructively, striving to achieve success in whichever milieu he found himself. From his introduction to the workplace a cook for KFC, Philippe enrolled in cosmetology school and soon went on to become a hair and makeup technician in the entertainment industry, which led him to the editorial sector of beauty industry publishing, which allowed him to become the first Beauty Editor for Upscale Magazine out of Atlanta, Georgia.

Despite his success as a beauty industry writer, Philippe felt another calling and it was at this critical juncture that he shifted from motivating people about their appearance to motivating them period. After taking this pivotal step, Philippe has not looked back—rather, he has grown and flourished as a multi-media motivational force.

Philippe launched a successful speaking career, traveling worldwide with his message of how to train the brain; eradicate the mental mindset and effects of generational poverty by initiating proactive personal and professional empowerment. Philippe also serves as a Personal Coach to private clients on a consultant basis which is where he developed the nickname "The SHOCKcoach," which is the acronym for Seeking Higher Omnipotent Conscious Knowledge!

The Official Launch of the Philippe Matthews Show

In 1999, he launched a highly successful ezine which gave him the impetus to launch the Philippe Matthews Show after being told by Mark Victor Hansen and many other mentors he should have his own TV show. The show originally premiered in local syndication in Chicago, January 2003 on CAN-TV 19 before the existence of YouTube in 2005 and ran for three years with a base audience of over 1 million viewers before launching on the internet in 2010.

Philippe's media career spans more than three decades with his first published in Sophisticates Black Hair Style Guide back in 1986. Since then he has been a mover and shaker in the areas of self-publishing, multimedia marketing, internet marketing and social media marketing. He is the owner of the SHOCKpublishing Group, Inc., and was featured on CNN's Financial News as an expert in the industry of ezine publishing and Internet Marketing.

Philippe Matthews is the author of the SHOCKwealth System: Developing the Mindset to Be Rich Before Becoming Rich; How to Make Millions When Thousands Have Been Laid Off featuring Stedman Graham and the SHOCKphilosophy: A Mindset for Massive Manifestation. His books and audio programs have been endorsed by Stedman Graham, Mark Victor Hansen, Dr. John F. Demartini, Robert G. Allen and countless more.

An internationally recognized internet marketer, writer, author, TV, radio host and one of the most trusted brands in alternative online media, his in-depth interviews capture the essence of what viewers are looking for in their quest for uncensored "HOW TO" information as well as what interviewees are looking for when sharing their message as well as what sponsors need when delivering a message to their customers.

Philippe Matthews has traveled the road of adversity, only to arrive at personal, professional and spiritual prosperity. It is the fruits of these very experiences that he shares with children and young adults across America and the world through the HOW Movement.

Honored by Mayor Richard M. Daley as a 'Principal for a Day' in the City of Chicago for three years, Philippe Matthews currently resides in Sacramento, California and enjoys wine tasting, fine cigars, and complimentary spirits!

The Social Sphere

Official Website
BlogTalk Radio
Twitter
Facebook
IMDB
About.me
Pinterest
Posterous
Youtube
iTunes
Linkedin
MySpace
Google Plus
Amazon.com Author Page

In The News

The Oprah of the Internet – Philippe Matthews on RonaldSpeaks
Philippe Shock Matthews on the Beverly Molander Show
Women's Radio with Nadine Lajoie

Other books by Philippe SHOCK Matthews

* *The Shock Philosophy: A Mindset for Massive Manifestation*
* *The Shock Theology Special Report: The Dark Side of New Thought Metaphysics & Religious Science*

RECOMMENDATIONS

Recommended Reading

The Philippe Matthews Show Blog

Dr. Dennis Kimbro on Secrets of Black Millionaires

Robert Kiyosaki on Why A Students Work for C Students

Kim Kiyosaki on Marriage, Money and Robert - p1 of 3

Lechter Answers and Reviews Who Took My Money – Part 1

An Exclusive Interview with Suze Orman on The Road To Wealth

Robert T. Kiyosaki on Wealth Mindset

Recommended Listening

The Philippe Matthews Radio Show

George Fraser on Power Networking

The Impact of Poverty on the Daddy Brain with Dr. Louann Brizendine

The ABCs of Money with Natalie Pace

John Perkins - Former Economic Hitman

Ryan Mack on Living in the Village

Recommended Viewing

The Philippe Matthews TV Show

Internet Marketing Technologist | Philippe SHOCK Matthews on CNN!

Mark Victor Hansen

Robert Kiyosaki

Dr. John F. Demartini

Robert G. Allen

Russell Simmons on Super Rich

Overcoming the Habit of Poverty with Dr. Brian King

Recommended Websites

The HOW Movement

The Philippe Matthews Show

Shock Author University Program

My Internet Marketing Expert

Recommended Social Media Sites

Twitter:

https://twitter.com/thepmshow

https://twitter.com/myiexpert

https://twitter.com/thehowmovement

Facebook:

https://www.facebook.com/thepmshow

https://www.facebook.com/TheHowMovement

https://www.facebook.com/myimexpert

BECOME A PART OF THE HOW MOVEMENT

Mission Statement

The mission and purpose of the HOW (Helping Ourselves Win) Movement teaches young adults how to empower, educate and train their brains to think like entrepreneurs and social change agents using The Exceptional Rules of Thinking(TM) in order to breakthrough the psychological, emotional, economic and environmental barriers of generational poverty that keep them from reaching their fullest potential.

Vision Statement

The Exceptional Rules of Thinking (TM) has been developed from personal and business life lessons along with in-depth interviews that Philippe Matthews has conducted with world class thought leaders, change agents and experts in the field of human potential. The HOW Movement will produce Internet TV, Radio, and Social Media Content that harnesses the intellectual, emotional and spiritual resources necessary for young adults to live an exceptional life and end the malady of generational poverty.

Quality Statement

Learning and deserving to live an exceptional life by training the brain to move from the mindset of why to why not. From victim to victorious. From poverty to wealth. From hope to HOW!

Daily Mantra

"I will strive to be exceptional in all I do. Regardless of my birthplace, environment, economic status, family or education; it is my birthright to achieve greatness and live an exceptional life!" -- Philippe SHOCK Matthews

Tagline

Moving from the illusion of Hope to the Process of HOW!

For more than 25 years, I have been researching the psychological effects of poverty and have made some startling connections that have been medically proven. 1) Children born in abject poverty, surrounded by gang violence, verbal/physical abuse, excessive bullying suffer from Severe Depression or _PTSD_, 2) PTSD weakens and comprises a region of the brain known as the _vmPFC_ (Ventromedial Prefrontal Cortex), 3) A compromised vmPFC creates _Learned Helplessness_, and 4) Learned Helplessness is the genesis of all addiction and bad habit formation.

This means, we have a society of people "addicted to poverty" because they were born into it and know of no way out! Children who live long enough to survive to see adulthood, suffer from PTSD just like our soldiers coming back from war; only worse. Troops coming back from war once knew what safety was. Kids and adults born in abject poverty and gang violent environments never get to develop that part of their brain that is able to recognize safety and make logical decisions for their future. ! I know this to be true because I am a product of abject poverty and was blessed to be able to get out alive and maintain a benevolent heart but not without severe pain and turmoil however.

I watched both my parents die within two months of each other right before my eyes when I was 14, I was only able to acquire a 6th grade education because I had to stay at home and take care of my mother, I was molested by my alcoholic father, I lived on welfare for years, I worked minimum wage jobs most of my young adult life, I lost all of my possessions and became homeless, I battled (still do) with an eating disorder, went through a crippling betrayal of my marriage that led to divorce and at the same time, I lost a $400,000 lawsuit from an unscrupulous network marketing company with zero dollars in the bank, the list continues!

Now, at age 47, I have lost half my life to the battle of poverty, now I dedicate the rest of my life to eliminating it and training the brains of young people to never have to live the life I have had to endure.

By the grace of God, there go I!

The only reason I did not become a statistic and/or a top news story on CNN is because of three promises *I made to my mother* which was 1) I will never do drugs, 2) I will never get involved in gang activity and 3) I will make something of my life that you would be proud of.

For decades now, I've been interviewing, studying and learning from the most brilliant minds in the world. Within the last ten years, I have aligned with some of the worlds leading scientists in the field of neuroscience and psychology to produce, develop and disseminate a powerful process to greatly reduce the effects of generational poverty, depression, Learned Helplessness and PTSD at the "brain" level using the HOW Movement's Programs.

WWW.HOWMOVEMENT.ORG

35% of the proceeds from this book will go to the HOW Movement!

www.ingramcontent.com/pod-product-compliance
Lightning Source LLC
Chambersburg PA
CBHW071247170526
45165CB00003B/1275